Fire the Phone Company:
A Handy Guide to Voice over IP

Dave Field

Peachpit Press

Fire the Phone Company: A Handy Guide to Voice over IP

Dave Field

Peachpit Press

1249 Eighth Street
Berkeley, CA 94710
510/524-2178
800/283-9444
510/524-2221 (fax)

Find us on the Web at www.peachpit.com.

To report errors, please send a note to errata@peachpit.com

Peachpit Press is a division of Pearson Education

Copyright © 2006 by Peachpit Press

Project Editor:
Kathy Simpson

Production Coordinator:
Jeff Sargent

Compositor:
Jerry Ballew

Indexer:
James Minkin

Interior design:
Charlene Will

Cover design:
Aren Howell

Notice of Rights

All rights reserved. No part of this book may be reproduced or transmitted in any form by any means—electronic, mechanical, photocopying, recording, or otherwise—without prior written permission from the publisher. For information on obtaining permissions for reprints and excerpts, contact permissions@peachpit.com.

Notice of Liability

The information in this book is distributed on an "As Is" basis, without warranty. While every precaution has been taken in preparation of this book, neither the author nor Peachpit Press shall have any liability to any person or entity with respect to any loss or damage caused or alleged to be caused directly or indirectly by the instructions contained in this book or by the computer software and hardware products described in it.

Trademarks

Many of the designations used by manufacturers and sellers to distinguish their products are claimed as trademarks. Where those designations appear in this book, and Peachpit was aware of the trademark claim, the designations appear as requested by the owner of the trademark. All other product names and services identified throughout the book are used in an editorial fashion only and for the benefit of such companies with no intention of infringement of the trademark. No such use, or the use of any trade name, is intended to convey endorsement or other affiliation with this book.

ISBN 0-321-38486-5

9 8 7 6 5 4 3 2 1

Dedication

This book is dedicated to:

My wife, Amy, and daughters, Marissa and Shaylee. You are my inspiration at 1 a.m. when the words won't come.

And to:

My father, Robert, who taught me why to work and who is prouder of my accomplishments than I am.

My mother, Nancy, who taught me everything I know about talking on the phone.

Acknowledgments

As with any project in which dozens of capable people come together to do something truly special, it is often difficult to know where to start. An undertaking like this is much more than the efforts of the person whose name graces the cover.

Let me start close to home:

Thank you, Amy, for your constant encouragement and understanding. You know I love this stuff, don't you?

Thanks, Marissa, for your earnest offers of help. I think you have a few good books in you, too!

Thank you, Shaylee, for making me play the Numa Numa Dance when I really wanted to work. You never let me take myself too seriously.

Also, let me thank:

Paul Marks and Dan Connor, for your assistance with art for Chapter 6. It is great to know there are those who are willing to help complete strangers in a bind.

Laura Lewin, my agent, without whom I would probably have chosen a new career by now.

Kathy Simpson, for translating all my works into English and for learning VoIP in the process.

Cliff Colby, for not getting twitchy when he saw a title beginning with the word *Fire*.

About the Author

By day, **Dave Field** is a mild-mannered systems engineer for a theme park in Bloomington, Minnesota. In this role, he has directed the installation of Camp Snoopy's entire network infrastructure. He has been the principal architect of point-of-sale implementations, ERP rollouts, and e-commerce initiatives.

After hours, Dave becomes an author, freelance trainer, and presenter. Certified MCSA and MCSE, Dave is expert at networking technologies and support-desk topics. He has delivered training at Microsoft Certified Technical Education Centers and has written content for Microsoft and Osborne/McGraw-Hill for the MCSE, MCSA, and MCDST certifications.

Dave's experience with Voice over IP began with softphones in 1996 and the MultiTech MultiVoIP hardware in 1999. He currently subscribes to more than a half-dozen VoIP services and is evaluating business telecommunications convergence solutions for Camp Snoopy.

Dave has written *How to Do Everything with Windows XP Home Networking* for Osborne/McGraw-Hill and *Installing, Configuring, and Administering Windows XP Professional (70-270)* (an academic textbook) for Microsoft Learning.

Contents

CHAPTER ONE What Is "Voyp"? 1
    The Birth of Internet Phones 2
    Internet Phone Basics 3
        Internet protocols 3
        VoIP protocols and codecs 4
        Internet phone devices 8
    The Big Picture 13
        Internet telephony resources 15
        More about VoIP standards 16
        Keep on reading 16

CHAPTER TWO Choosing Your Internet Phone Service 17
    A Tour of VoIP Providers 18
        Pure VoIP providers 18
        Established phone companies 22
        Cable companies 24
        Internet access providers with VoIP 26
        Softphone providers 27
    Evaluating the Available Offerings 30
        Selection criteria 30
        Using a decision grid to simplify selection 31
    Purchasing Your Service 33
        Selecting a service plan 33
        Choosing your equipment 34
        Considering installation assistance 36

CHAPTER THREE Planning for VoIP 37

    Assessing Your Infrastructure 39

        Got network? 39

        Let's look at the phones 40

        Identify your challenges 44

    Ready to Go? 52

CHAPTER FOUR Installing Your VoIP Equipment 53

    Getting Your Network Ready 54

        Connecting your TA with an Internet gateway 55

        Connecting without a gateway 56

    Installing a Telephone Adapter 57

        Connecting your TA 57

        Checking your work 58

        Safety concerns 59

    Installing a Combination TA/Gateway 60

        Connecting your gateway 61

        Testing Internet connectivity 64

        Configuring your telephone settings 66

        Connecting your phone 66

        Checking your work 66

        Safety concerns 67

    Installing Internet Phone with Cable Systems 67

        Getting started with digital phone services 67

        Managing digital phone distribution 68

    Installing Softphone Accessories 68

        USB handset installation 68

        Headphone installation 69

    Distributing the Telephone Signal 69

        First things first 70

        Connecting your TA to the distribution system 71

        Distributing telephone service without wires 75

    Summary 76

CHAPTER FIVE Setting Up Your Service 77

    Choosing a Purchase Option 78
        Retail purchase and activation 78
        Internet purchase and activation 78
    Activating Your Service 80
        A typical activation 80
        Your first call 82
    Postactivation Setup 83
        911 activation 83
        Local number portability (LNP) 86
        Calling-feature setup 88
        Additional lines 93
        Fax services 93
        Blended services 94
        Softphone service options 94
    Installing Softphone-Only Services 97
        Installing and configuring the Skype softphone service 97
        Integrate messaging and communications with Skype 100
    Testing Your Internet Phone 100
        Bandwidth testing 100
        Voice-quality testing 101
        Dealing with poor test results 102
    Bringing It All Together 103

CHAPTER SIX Common VoIP Problems and Their Solutions 105

    Connection Issues 106
        Bandwidth 106
        Intermittent connection loss 110
    Configuration Issues 112
        Gateway configuration 112
        TA configuration 116
    Hardware Problems 117
        TA failure 117
        Home wiring problems 118

Outages 121
    Power outage 122
    Internet and VoIP service outage 123
Additional Troubleshooting Resources 123

CHAPTER SEVEN VoIP Security 125

Security Q&A 126
    Will VoIP open my network to intruders? 126
    Can others eavesdrop on my phone calls? 127
    What other types of attacks are VoIP phones subject to? 127
    Can anyone steal my minutes? 129
    I use a wireless network. Is my VoIP secure? 129
Secure Your Internet Phone 131
    Analyze the risks 131
    Use a gateway 131
    Secure your wireless network 133
    Use encryption for direct calls 133
    Avoiding SPIT 134
Learn More about VoIP Security 135
    VoIP security resources 135
    VoIP security organizations 135

CHAPTER EIGHT Getting the Best Value from VoIP 137

The VoIP Value Equation 138
    More than unlimited minutes 138
    Virtual numbers 139
    Toll-free numbers 140
    VoIP direct saves even more 141
The Value of Convergence 142
    Integrated messaging 142
    Contact list integration 143
    Fax over Internet 144
    Multimedia communications 144

Finding Business Value with VoIP 145
    Business-to-business (B2B) VoIP 145
    A telecommuter's dream 145
    Essentially free for business 145
The Bottom Line 146
    Direct savings offer most compelling reason to switch 146
    Accessibility + integration + convergence = ROI 146

CHAPTER NINE Traveling with VoIP 147

Packing Your Bags 148
    What to bring 148
    Protecting your gear 150
    Avoiding an inquisition 150
    Your TA is in Phoenix?! 150
Finding Broadband 152
    Hotspots 152
    Hotels 154
    Business centers 155
    Wireless cities 156
    Using wireless Internet 157
Connecting to the Mother Ship 159
    Connecting your TA 159
    You did bring a handset, didn't you? 159
    Leaving the TA at home (or Phoenix) 160
Travel Safely 161
    Don't forget security 161
    Register your 911 service 162

CHAPTER TEN VoIP into the Future 163

Internet (Video)Phone 164
    Available today 164
    Coming soon 166

(More) Convergence 167
    Unified softphones 167
    Business convergence 169
Wireless VoIP 171
    Wi-Fi VoIP phones 171
    WiMax VoIP phones 172
Cellular and Wireless VoIP Combo Phones 173
    i-mate PDA2/PDA2k 173
    Motorola CN620 174

INDEX 175

Introduction

The door slammed as Alex Bell arrived home from school. He grunted a greeting to his mother as he passed the door to her office.

"How was your day, honey?" he heard her call as she rocked back in her chair.

Another grunt, and he was out of earshot. She heard the door to his room slam and a thump as his backpack hit the floor.

"I hope he took his laptop out first," she thought. Shrugging, she returned to her spreadsheet.

Alex had removed his laptop before the thump. He propped it open on his bed and pressed the power switch. While it booted, he went to his bathroom and splashed cool water on his face. It was hot this afternoon in Phoenix. He wondered—for the four thousandth time—why they had come here. After all, his mom could work anywhere.

By the time he returned to his room and grabbed a bottle of water from his mini-fridge, the laptop was booted, and Skype was online. He had several chat messages from friends and two voice mails. He could also see that 12 of his contacts were currently online. He spotted Tom Watson, his best friend in Phoenix. He Skyped him:

"Watson, come here. I want to see you!"

Not since Alexander Graham Bell uttered those same words in his laboratory in 1876 has communication changed to such a degree. We have broken the ties that bind our home phones to one incumbent local carrier and given consumers a choice of dozens of Internet phone companies.

With all the choices now available, it is necessary to have some knowledge of Internet phone technology to determine which company offers the best service. In this book, you will learn the basics of Voice over Internet Protocol (VoIP) and how this technology is used to deliver phone service to your

> **IN THIS INTRODUCTION**
>
> Chapter 1: What Is "Voyp"? **xii**
>
> Chapter 2: Choosing Your Internet Phone Service **xii**
>
> Chapter 3: Planning for VoIP **xii**
>
> Chapter 4: Installing Your VoIP Equipment **xii**
>
> Chapter 5: Setting Up Your Service **xiii**
>
> Chapter 6: Common VoIP Problems and Their Solutions **xiii**
>
> Chapter 7: VoIP Security **xiii**
>
> Chapter 8: Getting the Best Value from VoIP **xiii**
>
> Chapter 9: Traveling with VoIP **xiii**
>
> Chapter 10: VoIP into the Future **xiv**

home over a broadband Internet connection. You will learn how to choose among carriers based on features and functionality, how to look past the price to discern true value, and how to get the most from your Internet phone investment.

Here is a synopsis of what you will find in this book:

CHAPTER 1: WHAT IS "VOYP"?

This chapter provides a historical background on VoIP initiatives and technologies. You learn how VoIP is accomplished and are introduced to VoIP hardware and software.

CHAPTER 2: CHOOSING YOUR INTERNET PHONE SERVICE

This chapter introduces you to various Internet phone services. You will become familiar with various offerings and be able to make informed decisions about your service. I cover free and subscription services and local number portability, and I show you how to compare the array of available add-ons and features.

CHAPTER 3: PLANNING FOR VOIP

This chapter describes the setup options for VoIP in your home. You learn about broadband Internet requirements for VoIP and also where to place VoIP equipment for use with standard telephone handsets. You'll evaluate your current Internet service with an eye toward eventual VoIP installation.

CHAPTER 4: INSTALLING YOUR VOIP EQUIPMENT

This chapter helps you install and configure VoIP devices in the home. I show you where to find installation guides and resources for your particular service provider.

CHAPTER 5: SETTING UP YOUR SERVICE

In this chapter, you learn how to set up and test the actual VoIP service from your VoIP provider. I discuss methods of installation and ways to test the completed installation to insure call quality.

CHAPTER 6: COMMON VOIP PROBLEMS AND THEIR SOLUTIONS

In this chapter, you see how to solve some of the most common issues with a VoIP installation. Among them are insufficient Internet bandwidth for voice calls, configuration errors, and service errors.

CHAPTER 7: VOIP SECURITY

This chapter discusses Internet security in the context of VoIP implementations. I discuss privacy questions about VoIP calls that may arise and help you ensure that your Internet connection isn't inadvertently opened to hackers during the VoIP installation process.

CHAPTER 8: GETTING THE BEST VALUE FROM VOIP

Some VoIP providers allow you to provide "local" phone numbers to your family members and friends so that they can call you for free. I introduce these and other options to help you save even more money over toll-free and calling-card services for family and friends.

CHAPTER 9: TRAVELING WITH VOIP

Because Voice over IP uses the Internet to transport calls, you can use your phone any place you have access to a high-bandwidth connection. Take your phone service with you on vacation, and never miss a call! This chapter discusses how to travel with VoIP hardware and why a "softphone" on a laptop computer could be a better choice for some people.

CHAPTER 10: VOIP INTO THE FUTURE

VoIP technology continues to evolve. In this chapter, I present some coming advances and technologies. Specifically, I cover videophones and wireless VoIP phones, as well as late-breaking developments.

Take the chapters in order or à la carte, as your needs dictate. Tell your friends about Internet phones, and see the savings pile up!

Good luck with your new phone system, and many happy calls.

CHAPTER ONE

What Is "Voyp"?

You may have heard the term *Voice over IP, Voice over Internet Protocol,* or *VoIP* in discussions of Internet phones. You may even have some inkling that this term refers to the use of the Internet to transport your voice to another caller. After all the work you have done to get your computer on the Internet, phones would seem to be even more complex.

It really is not as complicated as it sounds. Although Internet protocols are inherently complex and require careful configuration, many Internet phone services take on the complex part of that setup and make phone service available to subscribers via preconfigured telephone devices. VoIP services have subscriber bases in the millions of users now and are successfully converting thousands of people to Internet telephony every day.

In this chapter, you will learn some of the basics of Internet phone technology and some important terms relating to this technology. After reading this chapter, you may not be able to carry on a conversation at a trade show, but you'll be able to hold your own in any water-cooler discussion of Voice over IP.

IN THIS CHAPTER
The Birth of Internet Phones 2
Internet Phone Basics 3
The Big Picture 13

The Birth of Internet Phones

Many of the elements of VoIP have been under development for many years. For example, G.711, the most widely used voice compression technology for VoIP, has been used since 1972 to pack more voice traffic onto long-distance telephone cables. If you use a digital ISDN phone at work, you are already using G.711. Other portions of the VoIP infrastructure, most notably the Internet itself, have been under development since the 1960s. VoIP is merely a conglomeration of many services into a cohesive package to enable business and consumer voice communications.

Enterprising developers began to tie these services together in the mid-1990s. In 1996, Net2Phone began offering computer-to-telephone communications over the Internet. The same year, VocalTec released the first computer-to-computer product for consumer VoIP, aptly named Internet Phone.

In 2000, Microsoft bundled Net2Phone's computer-to-phone product into its MSN Messenger product. Many users got their first taste of Voice over IP with this product. At the time, significant delays in speech transmission were common due to the relative scarcity of high-speed Internet services. Use of VoIP services required a firm commitment to save money, as the user would have to deal with noticeable delays in communication and the proper configuration of the computer's audio devices.

As new communication standards were ratified and came into use, VoIP continued to improve until, in January 2001, Vonage began offering VoIP solutions to business users. Business acceptance was a critical test for this technology, signaling the readiness of this technology for widespread use.

The VoIP industry has since grown to be the preferred communication solution for business call centers. Many companies now employ customer service and support representatives overseas, linking them to consumers with VoIP networks. One Microsoft Product Support Services representative once told me that Microsoft has call centers in nearly every world time zone, all using Voice over IP. In this way, the company can provide 24-hour support services while having staff work normal day-shift hours.

With all this growth, consumer VoIP remained a technology for propeller-heads until vendors began offering prepackaged solutions. As the larger VoIP players began offering these Internet phone kits, consumer acceptance accelerated. By early 2005, VoIP services in the United States passed the million-line mark. Analysts predict that by 2007, 30 percent of U.S. homes will be using this technology.

Internet Phone Basics

Internet phone systems use a collection of communication standards called *protocols* and *codecs* to carry out their mission of transporting your voice over the maze of cables and hardware that makes up the Internet. Some of these protocols control how your voice is broken up into pieces called *packets*; some conserve Internet bandwidth by compressing your communications; and some are responsible for making sure that your communication takes priority over less time-sensitive communications.

Manufacturers of Internet phone devices incorporate these protocols into their designs to create easy-to-use phones and telephone adapters for consumers and businesses. No knowledge of the inner workings of these protocols is actually required to use Internet telephone services, but basic knowledge can help you troubleshoot tricky error codes or configure certain settings for better performance.

Internet protocols

The Internet uses a suite of protocols to transport data from one point to another. These communication rules govern how computers (or phones) format data for transmission. In this section, I discuss protocols you may encounter while using Internet phones.

Common Internet protocols you may encounter during Internet phone configuration are

- *TCP/IP (Transmission Control Protocol/Internet Protocol)*. Most Internet communications use a suite of protocols collectively known as TCP/IP. TCP and IP combine to provide the infrastructure for voice data transmission.

  TCP/IP uses numeric addresses to route data between computers or devices connected to the Internet. Internet routers locate these addresses and plot the best route to use to deliver data to its destination. You may have seen these addresses when connecting your computer to the Internet.

- *UDP (User Datagram Protocol)*. A faster cousin of TCP, this protocol is often used for applications, such as voice transmission, in which speed is more important than reliability.

- *DHCP (Dynamic Host Configuration Protocol)*. This protocol controls Internet address assignment for many computers and devices that connect to the Internet. Devices that do not get their address from DHCP must have the address configured manually.

- *DNS (Domain Naming System)*. This term denotes both a protocol and a service by which hard-to-remember Internet addresses are translated into simpler addresses, like www.firethephoneco.com.

Many more Internet protocols are involved with Internet phone communications, but most work quietly behind the scenes to ensure priority routing for voice traffic or to maintain the Internet infrastructure by ensuring that traffic is rerouted around downed equipment.

VoIP protocols and codecs

VoIP uses a combination of methods for the conversion of voice to data that can be transmitted over the Internet. These methods can be broadly grouped into two groups: *Protocols* handle tasks such as voice session control and data transmission, and *codecs* manage the conversion and compression of voice into digital data.

VOIP SESSION PROTOCOLS

The primary use of protocols in VoIP is to establish and maintain a communication channel between two points. Protocols that perform this task are referred to as *session protocols*.

> **OTHER INTERNET TERMS YOU MIGHT ENCOUNTER**
>
> - *Host.* Any device having an address on an IP network such as the Internet.
>
> - *IP address.* A unique series of numbers that defines a host's address on the Internet. Many current IP addresses use a series of four three-digit numbers separated by decimal points.
>
> - *Packet.* A unit of data. Packets are created by splitting data into manageable pieces for transmission over a network.
>
> - *Ping.* An Internet troubleshooting utility that can be used to test the ability of the network to transmit data to its intended destination.
>
> - *Route.* The path a communication takes across the Internet.
>
> - *Router.* A device that directs Internet traffic toward its destination. Routers maintain address lists called *routing tables* that help them determine the best path to send data along. Another name for a router is a *gateway*.
>
> - *Server.* An Internet host that provides a service or information, such as the computer or computers that host a Web site.
>
> - *URL (Uniform Resource Locator).* An Internet address form that incorporates both the host address and the type of service the host is serving. In http://www.firethephoneco.com, for example, the http:// portion denotes a host serving the HTTP protocol (a Web server), and www.firethephoneco.com denotes the host's DNS address. Other URLs may begin with ftp:// (File Transfer Protocol) or sip:// (a host supporting direct voice communication).

The two most familiar VoIP session protocols are

- *SIP (Session Initiation Protocol)*. Most VoIP providers use this protocol to control VoIP session management. SIP establishes VoIP communication and controls most of the features of VoIP services. It includes everything required to manage features of VoIP that emulate the functions of a standard telephone, such as dial tone, ring tone, busy signal, and caller ID.

- *H.323*. A suite of telecommunication protocols that defines signaling and control in a manner similar to that of the SIP protocol. More mature than SIP, this standard is being replaced in many applications by the lighter, faster SIP.

VOIP TRANSPORT PROTOCOLS

Most VoIP communication is carried by the *Realtime Transport Protocol (RTP)*. After a communication is initiated by the VoIP session protocol, RTP acts as the carrier channel for voice data.

RTP was ratified as a standard in 1996 and has been used in VoIP and streaming audio/video services since then. It is designed to work with UDP (User Datagram Protocol) for maximum speed and efficiency.

OTHER VOIP SESSION PROTOCOLS

- *IAX (Inter-Asterisk eXchange)*. A protocol used by Asterisk, a private branch exchange (PBX) system that has Internet connection capabilities.

- *Megaco/MGCP (Media Gateway Control Protocol)*. A protocol that manages the conversion of voice data between networks or systems that have different protocols or codecs.

- *MiNet*. A proprietary protocol used by Mitel to manage its voice network products.

- *SCCP (Skinny Client Control Protocol)*. A proprietary protocol used by Cisco to manage VoIP sessions between Cisco equipment and compatible phones. SCCP is used mostly in business VoIP installations and probably will not be featured in a consumer VoIP environment.

VOIP CODECS

A *codec* (short for *compressor-decompressor*) manages the conversion of voice to digital bits and bytes. It is these algorithms that allow the dulcet tones of your voice to be faithfully reproduced at the other end of your Internet phone call. Codecs differ in the bandwidth they use; those that require less bandwidth typically reproduce less of the full range of voice tones. Some codecs reproduce tones well enough to be equivalent in quality to a good landline call; others are closer in quality to a cellular phone call.

Voice codecs in common use are

- *G.711*. The most common codec for VoIP communication, G.711 uses 64 Kbps to transmit high-quality voice and fax communications. Two versions of this codec exist: μ-*law* (pronounced "m-law"), used in the United States and Japan, and *a-law*, which is used in the rest of the world.

    The version of G.711 that you use becomes important because each region uses this protocol in its native version to compress voice on standard phone lines. Having the correct version ensures that the voice stream can be transmitted directly to the standard phone system without conversion.

> ### WAIT! HOW DO I KEEP ALL THESE ACRONYMS STRAIGHT?
>
> Relax! Take a deep breath.
>
> Better?
>
> Okay.
>
> For now, forget about the Internet protocol acronyms. You'll see them again when you need them. I'll make sense of them at the appropriate time.
>
> Of the VoIP session protocols, just remember SIP. Almost all providers now support the SIP standard. The H.323 standard is used mostly in commercial installations; the others are even more obscure.
>
> Most VoIP providers support more than one codec, G.711 being the most popular. Chances are that you will select your provider based on other factors, so I will discuss how to manage codecs at the appropriate time.
>
> So just relax, and enjoy a quick tour of VoIP hardware.

- *G.723.1.* This codec uses 5.3 Kbps to 6.3 Kbps of bandwidth (the lowest of the codecs I will examine in this book), making it useful for very-low-bandwidth VoIP applications such as VoIP over dial-up Internet. The voice reproduction quality is below that of G.711, and the codec is not suitable for fax transmission.

- *G.726.* Another low-bandwidth codec, G.726 can use as little as 16 Kbps or as much as 40 Kbps. At the lower settings, it may enable VoIP over dial-up Internet links. Quality is still less than that of G.711, however; therefore, this codec is not suitable for fax communication.

- *G.729.* A very-low-bandwidth codec in common use, G.729 uses as little as 6 Kbps to 8 Kbps to transmit voice data. Quality is less than that of G.711, but this codec remains a good choice for bandwidth-limited connections.

Internet phone devices

Consumers have an array of devices to consider as they evaluate VoIP services and options. Most VoIP providers specify a list of preconfigured devices for their services, but some, such as BroadVoice, allow clients to use any device compatible with their systems. For this reason, it may be important to understand the capabilities of various devices and to be able to analyze their compatibility with your chosen service. Most providers will also supply a list of compatible devices you can choose, many of them already configured for their services. Often, you can get the preconfigured device free or choose among a selection of device upgrades for a small fee. VoIP starter kits are also available at most retail computer stores; usually, these kits are free after rebates.

VoIP device manufacturers list the specifications of their devices on the packaging, and these specs usually appear on their Web sites as well (**Figure 1.1**). When evaluating a VoIP device, check to be sure that the device in question supports the same VoIP session protocol and codecs used by your service provider.

SIP PHONES

Many VoIP providers support one or more SIP telephone handset models. These devices look and feel like standard telephones but contain VoIP circuitry instead. Some can access the VoIP service directly through your Internet connection and are portable enough to travel with you when you want to take your home number on a trip.

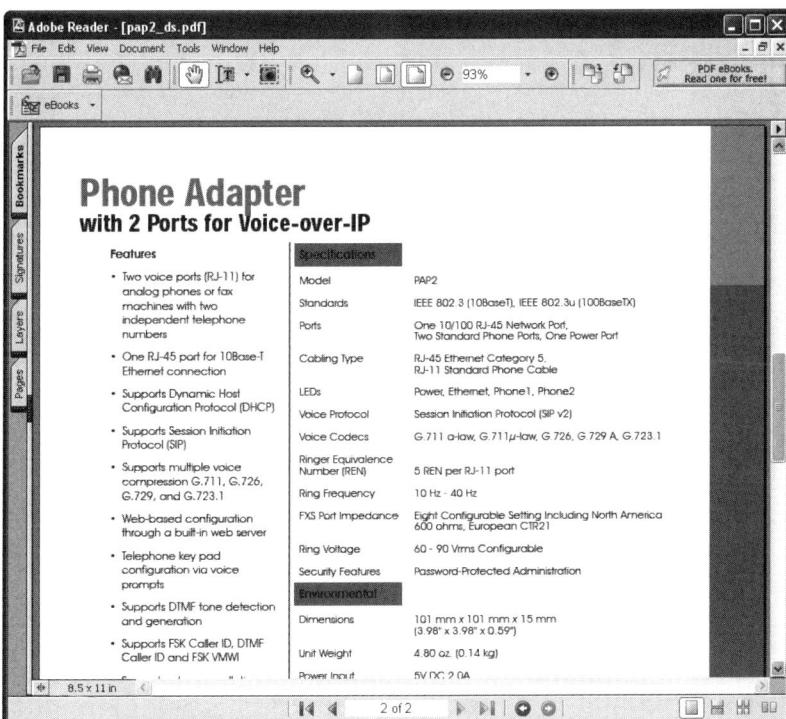

Figure 1.1 Product specifications for a Linksys telephone adapter

SIP phones come in three configurations:

- USB handsets connect directly to your computer, using its brains for network connectivity and signal processing (**Figure 1.2**). These devices are relatively inexpensive and work with many VoIP services. Most USB handsets are used with *softphones*—software telephone applications that use a computer to process voice codecs and VoIP protocols.

- SIP phone sets contain all the necessary circuitry for VoIP communication (**Figure 1.3**). These are desktop phones that look at home in an office environment. Manufacturers such as Cisco have many models to choose among.

- Wireless handsets use wireless networks in homes or offices to transmit data to and from the telephone handset (**Figure 1.4**). These devices look like common wireless handsets but contain all the circuitry for wireless VoIP.

SOFTPHONES

Many free and low-cost VoIP services use computer softphones (**Figure 1.5**). A softphone uses the computer's hardware to perform codec processing and protocol signaling, which dramatically lowers the cost of hardware for the user of these services. The softphone software may be created by the provider itself, as is the case with the Skype service, or the provider may use a custom-branded version of a softphone from a software supplier like XTen.

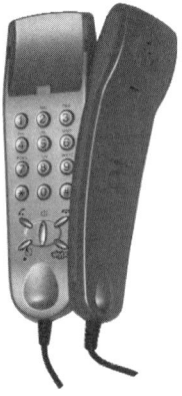

Figure 1.2 VoIPVoice CyberPhone K Skype USB handset

Internet Phone Basics   CHAPTER ONE   11

Figure 1.3 Cisco desktop VoIP phone

Figure 1.4 Cisco 7920 wireless VoIP handset

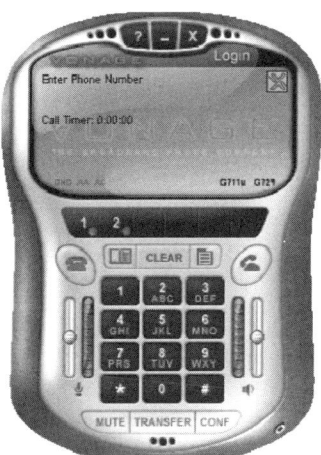

Figure 1.5 Vonage's SoftPhone is a custom-branded XTen softphone.

TELEPHONE ADAPTERS

Telephone adapters allow you to use a standard telephone to make VoIP calls (**Figure 1.6**). These devices convert the analog telephone signals to digital VoIP signals, using the selected VoIP session protocol and voice codec, and transmit these over your Internet connection to the VoIP provider's system.

Most telephone adapters, also called *TAs* or *PAs*, are supplied with starter kits for each VoIP provider, but they can also be obtained without presets for those who intend to use them for direct SIP-to-SIP communications or with a "bring your own device" provider like BroadVoice.

VOICE/DATA ROUTERS OR GATEWAYS

Many manufacturers of VoIP products also manufacture integrated appliances that contain the TA circuitry along with Internet gateway functionality (**Figure 1.7**). These devices can provide Internet connectivity to a home or small office, as well as VoIP capabilities. Many incorporate Internet firewalls and wireless networking features. They are a great way to reduce clutter on your desktop yet still have access to many communications services.

Figure 1.6 Linksys PAP2 telephone adapter

Figure 1.7 Linksys WRT54GP2 VoIP router/gateway

The Big Picture

VoIP devices, protocols, and codecs combine their roles to form the complete service you experience whenever you make an Internet phone call (**Figure 1.8**).

As you can see, you do not actually connect your phone to any telephone company's system. There is no requirement for you to remain in one place; in fact, you can be literally anyplace on Earth that has Internet connectivity and make a call as though you were right in your armchair at home. The called party will hear no difference (Internet connection quality being the

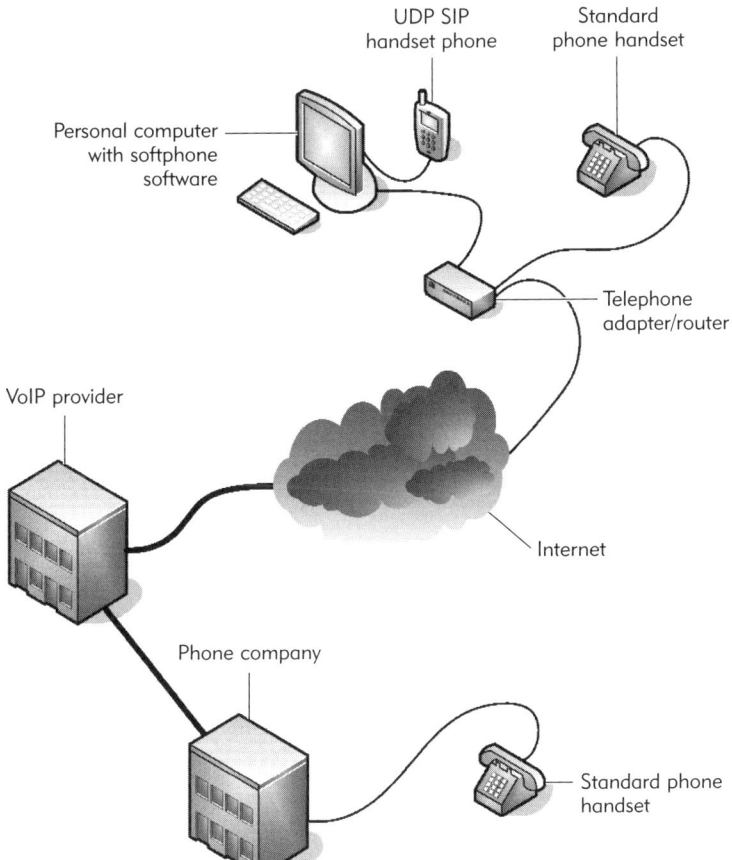

Figure 1.8 A typical Internet phone scenario

same), and you will continue to receive calls on your home number even while you're on vacation in Paris!

Imagine traveling with your local phone and being able to check in with friends and neighbors without the high-priced hotel phones or calling cards you typically use on a trip.

Follow an Internet phone call step by step as it is initiated by a VoIP caller (**Figure 1.9**):

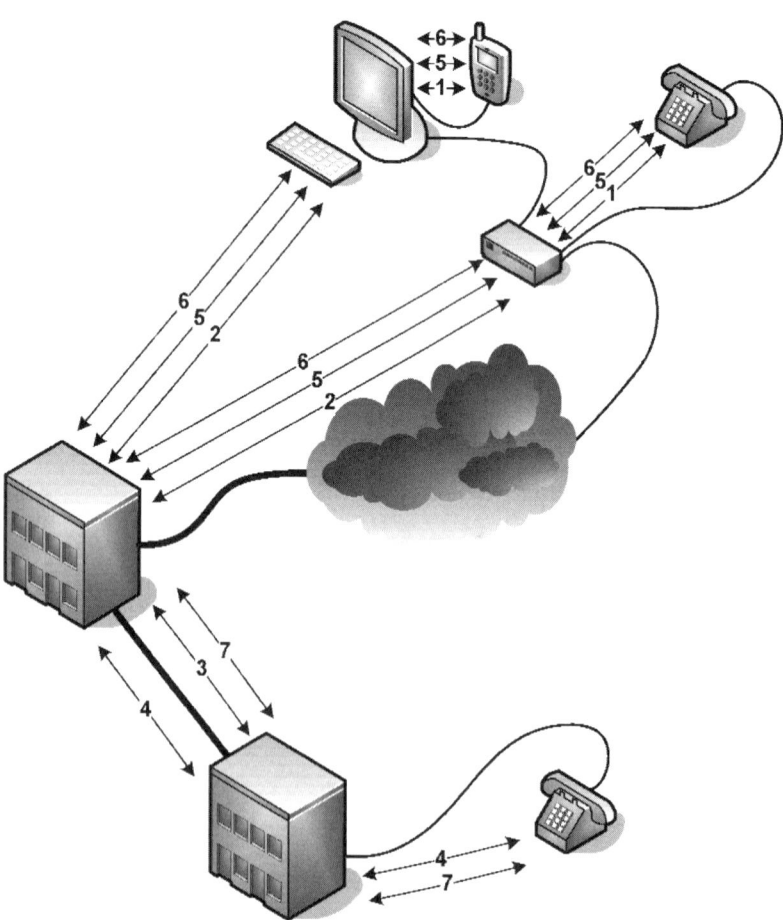

Figure 1.9 A VoIP call step by step

1. When a VoIP caller picks up a phone or initiates a call using a softphone, the VoIP session protocol signals the VoIP provider. The caller's TA (telephone adapter) generates a familiar dial tone. Then the caller begins to dial the number.

2. The tones of the phone handset are converted by the TA or the softphone software to a destination telephone number. The session protocol transmits this number to the VoIP provider.

3. The VoIP provider uses standard telephone signaling to access the correct line at the phone company.

4. The destination telephone begins to ring as the phone company transmits a ring-back signal to the VoIP provider.

5. The VoIP provider passes the ring-back tone to the caller via the VoIP session protocol.

6. When the called party picks up, the call is connected, and voice codec data begins to flow back and forth between the caller and the VoIP provider.

7. The VoIP provider translates this data to analog voice signals, which the phone company passes to the called party.

Internet telephony resources

Are you the type of person who needs to know more about your phone than just how to hook it up? Do you lose sleep wondering what makes it work or whether your conversations are truly confidential?

This section explores some VoIP resources you can use to learn more about VoIP technology, codecs, protocols, and standards. I'll list a few Web sites (mine included) where you can learn more.

If you could care less? Well, I'll see you in Chapter 2 in just a minute.

More about VoIP standards

VoIP standards are ratified by the International Telecommunication Union (ITU-T) and the Internet Engineering Task Force (IETF). Indeed, most of the codecs used in VoIP were created for use in traditional telephone systems. The SIP session protocol was ratified by the IETF and has been integrated with the ITU-T standards to allow interoperability. You can learn more about the standards behind VoIP at my Web site (www.firethephoneco.com), the Web site of the ITU-T (www.itu.int/itu-t), or that of the IETF (www.ietf.org). Especially interesting for those who need good bedtime reading is the IETF's SIP Request for Comments document, RFC 3261 (www.ietf.org/rfc/rfc3261.txt).

You can find a good discussion of VoIP codecs at the VoIP Wiki:

www.voip-info.org/wiki-Codecs

Keep on reading

Chances are that if your question hasn't been answered yet, it will be in the next several chapters, which discuss the evaluation, installation, and optimization of your Internet phone service. You'll use everything discussed in this chapter and more as you go through this process.

Let's rejoin the group now, shall we?

> **WHAT'S A WIKI?**
>
> *Wiki* is short for *wiki wiki*, which means *quick* in Hawaiian. A *wiki* is a user-managed online information forum. Users can register to contribute to articles, refining the content and meaning of items that they specialize in. In addition to the VoIP Wiki, other popular wikis are
>
> - Wikipedia (www.wikipedia.org). One of the largest wikis in existence. With more than 500,000 articles in more than 20 languages, Wikipedia is one of the most complete online encyclopedias.
> - Portland Pattern Repository Wiki (http://c2.com/cgi/wiki) The first wiki. This site is still the best source for wiki information and history. Many folks learn to wiki here.

CHAPTER TWO

Choosing Your Internet Phone Service

For the first time in history, you actually can choose the phone company that will serve your home. Telecommunications deregulation made some choice available, but that was nothing like the explosion of choices you see now. Chances are that your phone company, your cable company, and (in some communities) even your power company can make your home phone ring. Add to this the hundreds of Voice over IP phone companies, and the choices are staggering. In this chapter, you will tour the most common choices and learn the pros and cons of each. You will gain insight into how each service operates and be able to ask the right questions to find the service that is right for you.

IN THIS CHAPTER
A Tour of VoIP Providers **18**
Evaluating the Available Offerings **30**
Purchasing Your Service **33**

A Tour of VoIP Providers

Before you can make an informed selection of an VoIP provider, you should know what is available to you. Providers approach VoIP from many directions, and each has its own unique pros and cons. This section looks at the major players in the VoIP industry. Keep in mind that some of these options may not be available in your area. After the tour, I will discuss some of the criteria you might use when making your selection.

Pure VoIP providers

First to the table were the pure VoIP providers. This is all they have ever done, and most of them are very good at what they do. They have spent more than a decade tweaking their systems for the best call quality and are a very good choice for most VoIP installations. Their systems are configured to make use of common Internet connection methods and do not force you to choose a specific type of Internet connection.

Providers in this category typically offer free or subsidized telephone adapters and reasonably priced service plans. Many also offer free or low-cost international dialing to selected countries.

Many providers in the category have the ability to add virtual numbers to your service. *Virtual numbers* allow you to add a number in the same area code as a friend, family member, or business associate to let them call you without long-distance charges. One provider (BroadVoice) even goes so far as to offer local numbers in the United Kingdom. With this option, relatives and friends in England, Scotland, Wales, and Ireland can call these numbers for free, ringing your phone in the United States.

EVALUATING A PURE VOIP PROVIDER

Because most major Pure VoIP providers offer technically equivalent VoIP technologies, they compete mostly on features and price. There are some minor differences with regard to the use of codecs and system reliability. You can find out more about these differences by using a resource such as the providers' Web sites to identify the codec in use. For questions about quality, Broadband Reports offers a VoIP service ranking on its Web site (www.broadbandreports.com).

You may know someone who has experience with one ore more of these services. That person would be a good source of information on the quality of customer service offered by his or her provider and on the frequency and length of outages in your area.

Table 2.1 lists some pure VoIP service providers. This list is by no means complete; a Google search for "home VoIP" will uncover hundreds of services operating in this market. These are providers that have been most active recently and that have generated the most positive buzz about their services.

Table 2.1 Major Pure VoIP Providers		
Provider Name	**Web Address**	**Phone**
BroadVoice	www.broadvoice.com	978-418-7300
Broadvox Direct	www.broadvoxdirect.com	800-273-9134
Lingo	www.lingo.com	866-546-4603
Net2Phone	www.net2phone.com	877-627-4663
Packet8	www.packet8.net	888-898-8733
QuantumVoice	www.quantumvoice.com	800-914-2943
SunRocket	www.sunrocket.com	800-786-0132
VoicePulse	www.voicepulse.com	732-339-5100
Vonage	www.vonage.com	877-486-6001

DETERMINING SERVICE AVAILABILITY

Pure VoIP providers broker deals with local telephone carriers to get access to blocks of phone numbers in certain areas. They use these numbers to assign you a number that is local to callers in your community. You can find out whether a provider has local numbers in your area by using the availability tools on the provider's Web site or by calling its sales number.

If the VoIP provider has not yet made an agreement with a local carrier, you may be offered a number from a neighboring community. Be sure to check whether this number is a local call in your community. If the lack of local numbers is not an issue for you, you can still obtain service; you just won't get a local number.

LOCAL NUMBER PORTABILITY (LNP)

Many VoIP providers will attempt to transfer your existing telephone number to your new service. This process is called *local number portability (LNP)*. This transfer can take some time to accomplish, and your phone service

> **DISCONNECTING DSL**
>
> When your LNP is carried out successfully, your current service will be disconnected. If you have DSL Internet services on the affected line, they will most likely be stopped at the same time. To avoid this situation, you can use a DSL service that does not require a local line (not available in all areas), switch your DSL to another line, or switch your Internet connection to a local cable or wireless Internet provider.

> **PROBLEMS WITH LOCAL NUMBER PORTABILITY**
>
> Local number portability was originally ordered by the Federal Communications Commission to allow cellular phone companies to transfer a customer's existing phone number to their services. Whether the transfer was from terrestrial phone to cellular phone or cellular to cellular, this service let subscribers obtain new service without going through the hassle of changing phone numbers.
>
> VoIP providers also use this service to transfer numbers to their systems but must use the services of a competing local exchange carrier to wrest the numbers from the original providers. If the providers do not have a carrier in your community or are stonewalled by the local telephone company, they might not be able to transfer your number.
>
> VoIP providers are lobbying for the same LNP access as that enjoyed by the cellular carriers, but this may take some time to iron out.

that is using the number will be disconnected during that time. This can be an issue if you also have DSL Internet associated with this line, so be careful when activating this feature.

VoIP providers occasionally have difficulties transferring a number or may not be able to transfer it at all. When this happens, you will be given the choice of receiving a new number or canceling your service.

VOIP BLOCKING

Some pure VoIP providers have run into issues with local Internet providers. There have been documented cases in which a local Internet provider (which happens to have its own VoIP service) has blocked the VoIP traffic of a competing VoIP provider's subscribers. The Federal Communications Commission (FCC) has had to become involved in a few cases and has levied fines against the local providers.

USING 911 SERVICES WITH VOIP PHONES

Access to 911 services is currently a hot topic in the VoIP community. Certain high-profile cases have prompted all carriers to examine their 911 offerings. Some providers did not even offer 911 dialing and recommended that customers use a cellular phone to access emergency services. For many consumers, this situation was simply not acceptable. Imagine your babysitter or a family member attempting to call 911 and not getting through. Life and property are more important than saving a few dollars on your phone bill.

In May 2005, the FCC heard testimony about the options and challenges of VoIP 911 services. VoIP operators were lobbying for direct access to the 911 infrastructure, while some local carriers resisted that notion, claiming that they had invested much in the infrastructure and did not want to share it. Finally, testimony from customers who had bad experiences with the so-called 911 services that had been put together by VoIP operators moved the FCC to order incumbent local carriers to allow VoIP operators access to their 911 infrastructures.

Continued on next page

> **USING 911 SERVICES WITH VOIP PHONES** *Continued*
>
> This process continues. Some VoIP providers are closer to the goal than others. Some have improvised solutions to provide interim 911 access to their customers. Possibly the best interim solution is that employed by Level 3 Communications. The company employs a technique called *direct trunking*, in which it creates its own connection to the 911 dispatch centers through terrestrial phone lines. Callers using that system can be assured that their full name and address information will be transmitted to the 911 dispatcher during an emergency call.
>
> The bottom line about 911 is to test it on the service you eventually choose. Dial 911, and when an operator answers, immediately inform him or her that this is not an emergency and that you are verifying the ability of your Internet phone to access emergency services. Ask the operator whether he or she received your name and address information with your call. As soon as you have assessed the operator's ability to assist you in the event of an emergency, thank him or her, and hang up. Keep the call short, and do not attempt to engage the operator in a long-winded discussion about your brand-new phone. Also, avoid calling during a hurricane warning or other known busy time for these personnel. If you receive a brusque response, do not take it personally. These lines are for emergencies, and operators are trained to end nonemergency calls quickly.

Established phone companies

Not to be outdone, many traditional phone companies are now offering VoIP service. Some companies offer VoIP as part of a complete package of phone, DSL Internet, and television programming. Because they own the wires to your home, they are in a position to offer significant savings on these communications bundles.

Although it may seem counterproductive for a phone company to offer VoIP when it owns the phone wires, it makes sense if the local provider continues to enjoy your business, or when the provider wants to slip over the border and start signing up a competitor's customers. In fact, one of the most visible

VoIP providers—AT&T CallVantage—seeks to offer VoIP telephone access in competition with your traditional phone company.

There are significant pros and cons to this approach. Established providers of telephone services (and who is more established than AT&T?) have access to insider information and can perform local number portability effectively when others cannot. In addition, these companies have huge investments in infrastructure and own most of the network that will carry your voice data. This gives them better control of the quality of the service you receive.

On the other hand, these companies are firmly entrenched in the business of telecommunications, and you may feel that they have had their day. Also, many consumers feel that the large telecommunications providers are not focused enough on providing good customer service.

EVALUATING ESTABLISHED PHONE COMPANIES

When evaluating the services provided by established phone companies, you will consider many of the same aspects of service that you would with a pure VoIP provider. Codec, call quality, and service ratings, for example, are just as important for phone companies as they are for pure VoIP providers. You can also use the companies' Web sites to check for service availability in your area.

As you can for pure VoIP providers, you can find rankings of service quality for these providers. Hold established phone companies to the same standards of service that you would expect from the startups, and you should be able to make an informed decision about the suitability of their services. **Table 2.2** lists phone companies that have announced VoIP offerings.

Table 2.2 Established Phone Companies Offering VoIP Service

Provider Name	Web Address	Phone
AT&T CallVantage	www.callvantage.com	866-816-3815
Qwest OneFlex	www.qwest.com/residential	800-899-7780
Verizon VoiceWing	www.verizon.com	800-270-5369

DETERMINING SERVICE AVAILABILITY

Established telecommunications companies must still make deals with local telephone carriers to get access to blocks of phone numbers. They use these numbers to assign you a number that is local to callers in your community. You can find out whether the provider has local numbers in your area by using the availability tools on its Web site or by calling its sales number. If the company you are evaluating happens to be your local carrier, it will definitely have more flexibility with numbers than other companies will.

Availability of 911 services varies with these providers. Be sure to read their 911 access statements carefully so that you know what to expect.

Cable companies

In a bid to expand their revenue, many cable companies first began offering broadband Internet service and now offer phone service. Phone services with cable companies may differ significantly from what you may have come to expect with Voice over IP. Some cable companies simply add a telephone adapter to their broadband service; others install a completely separate solution requiring network interface units (NIU) to be installed on the side of your home. Still others use an expanded set-top box to provide telephone services. Whatever the solution, it will be specific to the cable company's infrastructure and will almost certainly require its own equipment to establish service.

That is not to say that cable telephone services are not desirable. Many cable phone services offer very good call quality and competitive rates. Just compare them with your other VoIP options to be sure that you are getting the best value for your money. Do not be tempted by "single bill" offers unless you can be assured that they offer you bottom-line savings.

EVALUATING CABLE TELEPHONE PROVIDERS

The task of evaluating a cable telephone provider is simplified by the fact that you will likely only have one choice. You may also discover that the cable company representative cannot or will not provide information about voice codec or service reliability. That said, although cable companies are notorious for their unreliability, the telephone systems are built on their newest equipment and best cables. You are likely to have a good experience with this technology. Cable providers also have the advantage of better access to the 911 infrastructure and, therefore, have a higher likelihood of being able to provide the enhanced 911 services that you have come to expect from the local phone company.

Ask for a trial period to use the service and verify its quality. Many providers will provide the service on a 30-day money-back guarantee. This way, you can test it before committing yourself to a long-term contract.

THE EFFECT OF CABLE OUTAGES

Many people are concerned that a cable outage will also take down their phone service. This is a possibility but not a certainty. Cable companies use separate equipment to process cable and telephone service, and the two services are combined on a single cable only when they get near your home. For this reason, unless there is a cable break or storm damage, your phone service should continue to operate even during "technical difficulties" on the television side. Often, the phone equipment will also be supplied with backup power, keeping your service online even during a power outage.

DETERMINING SERVICE AVAILABILITY

You will need to contact your local cable operator to determine whether it offers VoIP services. For large operators, you can do this by accessing the companies' Web sites and using their availability tools. You may have to contact a smaller operator by phone. Service may depend on your location within the company's infrastructure, as the company may not have had sufficient demand to build out to your area yet. If a cable company does not currently offer VoIP service, ask to be placed on a list to be notified when it becomes available. This is how cable companies track demand, and it may encourage them to move into your area sooner.

Many cable operators can offer excellent 911 services because they employ Level 3 Communications' 911 services. When you evaluate cable companies' offerings, be sure to read any statements about 911 dialing carefully so that you know what to expect. Call the customer-service department if you are not sure.

Internet access providers with VoIP

Who could possibly know more about Internet technologies than an Internet access company? These companies have existed in one form or another since the commercialization of Internet access began in the early 1990s. Many large Internet providers now offer telephone service as one of their products. This service is a natural fit for them, as it uses their own infrastructure for distribution and they have direct control of the quality and reliability of the service.

EVALUATING AN INTERNET ACCESS PROVIDER

Traditionally, people tend to change Internet providers as often as they change hairstyles (more often, in my case). If you are planning to tie your voice services to your Internet bill, you may have to resist the Internet access revolving-door habit. Many Internet access providers require you to use their Internet service to activate voice service.

Internet access providers that offer telephone service may resell the services of a larger telecommunications provider, such as Level 3. This allows them to provide access to Voice over IP to their customers without the expense of building the infrastructure themselves. They will act as the local collection point for calls, sending them over the larger provider's network and receiving a portion of the service fees in return. In fact, providers such as Level 3 do not sell their services directly to consumers, so this may be the only way to access these reliable services.

Be sure to ask the same questions you would of a pure VoIP provider. Determine which codecs the companies support and whether they offer local number portability. **Table 2.3** lists national Internet access providers that offer VoIP services.

Table 2.3 National Internet Access Providers with Telephone Service

Provider Name	Web Address	Phone
America Online (AOL)	www.aol.com	800-881-9832
EarthLink Unlimited Voice	www.unlimitedvoice.com	866-866-2434
Speakeasy	www.speakeasy.net	800-890-5214

DETERMINING SERVICE AVAILABILITY

Your Internet access provider's Web site can tell you whether the company offers VoIP service in your area. If the site does not have an availability tool or a map, call the customer-service line to ask about availability. The Web site or customer-service representative should also be able to tell you which equipment is required or provided with your service. Be sure to inquire about 911 dialing and access to emergency service personnel.

Softphone providers

The very first Internet phones were computers running programs that translated voice into bits and bytes for transmission over the Internet. So-called softphones are still very much in use on the Internet today. In fact, the largest subscriber bases of any VoIP service are recorded on the free softphone services. Foremost among these are Skype and Free World Dialup. With tens of millions of callers using their networks every day, these services are connecting callers globally on a scale never seen before. Recent reports have Skype supporting more than 2 million concurrent calls during some periods. Imagine the populations of two largish cities all speaking to one another at the same time!

Softphones are computer programs that you download and install on your computer system. Most providers have versions that run equally well on Windows, Macintosh, and Linux PCs. All you need are the computer, a sound card, and a microphone. Some services, such as Skype, can also use USB handsets like those discussed in Chapter 1. These handsets allow you to access the functions of the Skype application by using the handset's keys.

> **NOTE**
>
> Macintosh users may discover that handsets are limited to producing sound. Not all softphone software is capable of presenting full functionality to OS X users.

You can even browse your address book and select the party you want to call (**Figure 2.1**)!

CONSIDERATIONS FOR SOFTPHONE USE

The first consideration for use of softphone VoIP is whether you have the appropriate infrastructure. Obviously, you need a computer to access these services, and the computer should be capable of running the software efficiently. The softphone provider's Web site should list the hardware requirements for its application. Ensure that your system meets these minimum standards.

You should also realize that you will be tied to your computer during any softphone call. Because this service requires your computer's processing power and sound card, you can roam only as far as the cable reaches, and your computer must remain powered on for you to make and receive calls.

Unless you subscribe to a softphone provider's premium service level, you will not receive a phone number at which terrestrial phone callers can reach you. Options like SkypeIn from Skype offer this service, but at prices comparable with those of pure VoIP providers.

Most calls on softphone networks are *peer-to-peer*—that is, they are made directly from one computer to another. This allows the softphone provider to act only as a directory of connected users and not be required to maintain a massive communications infrastructure.

Softphone networks are geared to more advanced users. Typically, you will not receive direct technical support; rather, you must receive support from other users in the community or via e-mail.

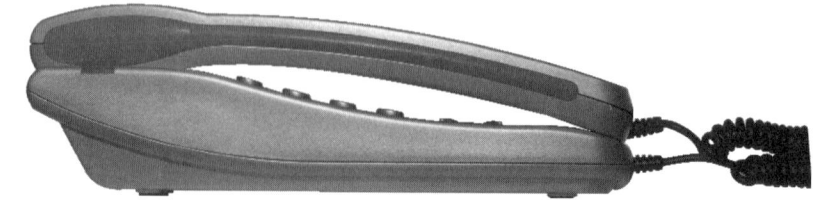

Figure 2.1 This USB handset from VoIPVoice is optimized for use with the Skype phone service.

EVALUATING SOFTPHONE VOIP PROVIDERS

Softphone VoIP is a different animal from the service offered by a provider that uses telephone adapters. Because the provider uses its own software application, it is up to the provider how to process and transmit voice data. Providers are free to use standard telephony codecs or not. Skype, for example, uses proprietary coding and encryption, and is not compatible for direct connectivity with any other service. Skype users can call terrestrial phone and VoIP users by using the SkypeOut option but cannot make direct calls to users of Free World Dialup.

When evaluating softphone services, you usually just need to install and use the pertinent applications. Because many of these services are free, you are under no obligation to buy anything unless you want to try premium features. You may have more than one of these applications installed on your computer but may experience problems if two or more are active at the same time.

Table 2.4 lists some of the better-known softphone VoIP providers.

Table 2.4 Softphone VoIP Providers

Provider Name	Web Address	Phone
Pulver Free World Dialup	www.pulver.com/fwd	N/A
Skype	www.skype.com	N/A
Voiceglo	www.voiceglo.com	N/A

DETERMINING SERVICE AVAILABILITY

Softphone providers are global in nature. Unless you are using an optional add-on to receive calls, you will not be concerned about availability beyond having sufficient bandwidth for the service. If you are using an optional inbound call service, you will need to find out whether a provider has numbers in your area. Use the availability tool on the provider's Web site for this purpose.

Evaluating the Available Offerings

Now that you've been introduced, it's time to get to know your providers better. In this section, I lay out an evaluation methodology that you can use to select the best provider for your needs. It is a simple decision matrix I like to use when making selections in my line of business. It helps me prioritize important factors and not get lost considering the minor differences of the services or products I am evaluating.

In the following paragraphs, I list several selection criteria for a VoIP service. Prioritize these criteria based on your own needs and use them to evaluate your available service offerings.

Selection criteria

I could name a hundred items that you could take into account when choosing a service provider. "Does it have caller ID?", you may ask. Almost all providers do. So many features are available, in fact, that evaluating the competing services on a feature-by-feature basis is nearly impossible. It is very easy to catch featuritis and get lost in a comparison of (truthfully) inconsequential features.

Criteria such as the availability of local numbers, virtual numbers, and 911 service might be important to you. If so, make sure that they take precedence over the less important features.

CALLING FEATURES

There may be one or more calling features you enjoy in your current phone service that you prefer not to live without. If you conference-call a lot, you will want to make sure that three-way or conference calling is available. Voice mail and caller ID are other common features that most users appreciate.

Try not to get caught up in details about features you do not need or will not use. Providers often try to impress by counting their features for you. Look beyond that to the features you will actually use.

LOCAL NUMBER AVAILABILITY

Some providers may not yet offer numbers in your local calling area. You'll want to make sure that local callers do not incur a toll charge when they call you. If you cannot get a number that is free to your local callers, you might be inclined to evaluate other offerings.

ADDITIONAL (VIRTUAL) NUMBERS

Many VoIP providers offer the ability to activate additional numbers in other parts of the world. This allows you to give your friends, family members, or business associates toll-free local phone numbers that ring on your home phones. This is a great way to allow your parents (or children) to call you for free.

911 AVAILABILITY

Even though the FCC directed VoIP providers to provide Enhanced 911 service in May 2005, some providers have progressed farther than others in this process. Many providers are beginning to partner with incumbent carriers for access to 911 infrastructures in many areas, but much remains to be done. Be sure to check with the companies you evaluate to see where they are in this process.

Using a decision grid to simplify selection

Begin by selecting five to seven features or aspects of VoIP that you consider important to your service. I list a few in the following grid; feel free to add to the list as you become more familiar with these services. If you discover a feature you like in one service and consider it critical to your evaluation, be sure to add it to the list.

Weight each feature by assigning it a number according to its relative importance to you. This allows you to score each service, identifying the combination of features and cost that best fits your needs. Use a grid similar to the one below to record your rankings. Record a score for each provider, multiplying your opinion of the service (on a scale from 1 to 10) by the weight factor. Record the weighted score in the grid. (In the grid below, the weighted score is in parentheses.) Total the weighted score numbers to obtain each provider's total score.

It is easy to see the effect of weighting the features according to their relative importance. If 911 service is most important to you, you would accept Provider 1, even though it might fall behind on local number portability and international rates. Provider 3 also makes a strong showing, simply because it has reasonable 911 service.

By the way, did you notice that codecs and VoIP protocols didn't even come into the discussion? Picking a plan is a very subjective exercise, and the closest the grid comes to codec consideration is call quality. This might change later, when you begin installing and optimizing your service, but for now, it is properly placed in the realm of the propellerheads.

Feature	Weight Factor	*Provider 1*	*Provider 2*	*Provider 3*
Virtual numbers	8	9 (72)	9 (72)	7 (56)
Low international rates	6	8 (48)	8 (48)	6 (36)
911 service	10	10 (100)	0 (0)	8 (80)
Call quality	8	7 (56)	9 (72)	8 (64)
Consumer reputation	7	9 (63)	8 (56)	8 (56)
Local number portability	6	5 (30)	8 (48)	7 (42)
Your addition		Score (weighted score)	Score (weighted score)	Score (weighted score)
Provider totals		369	296	334

Purchasing Your Service

After selecting the service provider that is the best fit for your priorities, you will want to get on board with its service plans and equipment. Fortunately, this is the easiest part. Not one of these providers would be in business if it made buying its services hard. A few Web forms or a few minutes on the phone, and you are done!

Take note that you have not even considered service plans until now. This is because the most important part of the selection is the feature set, not the minutes. Most providers will zip you right to the service-plan selection, completely glossing over the technical underpinnings of their services. You may soon become disenchanted with the actual performance of the service and take off to find another, perhaps paying a substantial early-cancellation penalty as you leave. By shopping for features first, you eliminate this revolving-door experience. If you are satisfied with the features and quality of your service, you might even be willing to pay slightly more for it.

In the next section, I discuss the selection of service plans, equipment, and installation support.

Selecting a service plan

Assume for a moment that you have selected your service provider. Now it is time to drive a hard bargain by deciding which of the provider's service plans best serves your needs. As you have probably already discovered, there is not much in the way of bargaining to do; you choose the basic, middle, or deluxe plan. "Good, Better, Best" is classic marketing. Show clients a progression, and they will go deluxe every time.

Take a close look at what you are getting. If you never use more than 300 minutes of calling time per month, and most of it is domestic long distance, why opt for the "Unlimited World Domination" plan? You might be better off with a 300-minute plan with low rates for additional minutes.

Read the details of each plan carefully to see how it applies to your real-world situation. Buy the one that gives you the best value for your pattern of use.

Choosing your equipment

Most VoIP providers offer a free telephone adapter or network interface unit for their services. You might be able to choose other optional equipment. These devices usually cost a bit more but may be well suited to your situation.

If you wander about during calls, you might choose the wireless handset option offered by your provider. If you do not have a broadband router, you might choose to purchase the router with integrated phone ports. Look over the available options, and select the device that best serves your needs.

BRING YOUR OWN DEVICE (BYOD)

Some services allow you to use your own telephone adapters and IP phones. If you currently have one of these devices, check your provider's ability to support compatible codecs and protocols. If they allow BYOD, most providers offer you the choice to use your own equipment on the device-selection page of their sign-up process (**Figure 2.2**). You often receive a discount on your service-activation fee if you use your own equipment.

RETAIL STARTER KITS

Some providers also offer retail startup kits for purchase at major computer retailers. With the purchase of one of these kits, it is possible to buy and activate your service in a single day. If this option appeals to you, be sure you select your provider before you enter the store. Standing there staring at two kits is not the time to make this decision. (My apologies to those who picked this book up from the rack next to their starter kits.)

Starter kits usually include a telephone adapter or broadband router with voice ports (**Figure 2.3**), cables for connecting to your computer and Internet service, and a quick-start guide. By following the instructions in the guide, you can install and activate your service in as little as 15 minutes.

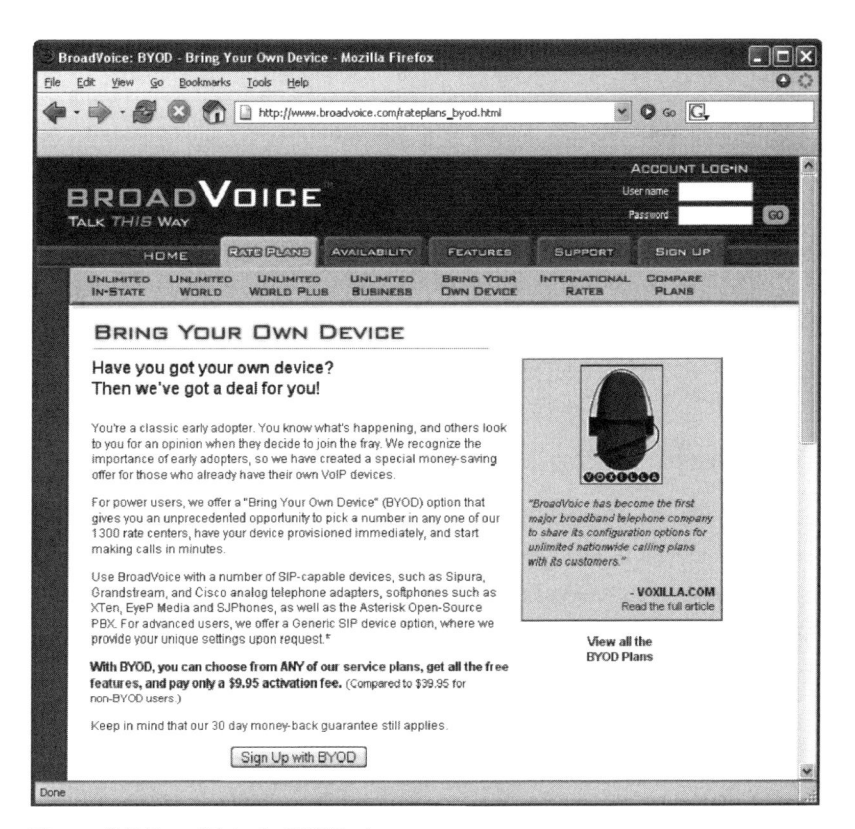

Figure 2.2 BroadVoice's BYOD sign-up page

Figure 2.3 The D-Link DVG-1120 is provided with some AT&T CallVantage starter kits.

PREACTIVATED DEVICES

If you choose to sign up online, the device you select will usually be preactivated by your VoIP provider. When you receive the device, all you have to do is plug it in. This can simplify installation, especially for those who really dread making network devices talk to each other. Preactivated hardware is also more likely to be up to date with regard to device programming for best reliability and performance. Retail starter kits may have been on the shelf for a while and might need a firmware update (discussed in Chapter 6) to fix minor performance and stability issues.

Considering installation assistance

Most VoIP providers can assist you with setup and configuration of your service. Often, this involves a telephone support call to make sure that everything is installed and connected correctly. Retail stores may offer to install your retail starter kit for a fee. If you are not technically inclined, this might be an excellent option for you. The store will send a technician out, and he or she will leave you with a functioning telephone service.

Cable providers often require you to use their professional installation services. If this is the case, hold out for free or discounted installation. If you stick to your guns, the sales representative will often throw it in as a sign-up incentive. Just be sure to mention that you are considering other VoIP services as well.

Softphone providers usually do not offer installation assistance, but you can find many helpful folks in their online forums who can assist you with your service. These online communities are frequented by some very generous and helpful people. Be sure to thank them publicly in the forums unless they request that you refrain from doing so.

Lest you despair, don't forget that Chapter 4 is coming up soon. That chapter gets into network hookups and installation of VoIP devices in depth and should answer any questions you still have at this point.

CHAPTER THREE

Planning for VoIP

Some Internet phone setups fail to impress because easy-to-discover problems exist in the configuration of the telephone adapter or the Internet connection. Checking these problems out before installation could have made the project more successful and the subscriber's first experience with VoIP much more satisfying.

IN THIS CHAPTER
Assessing Your Infrastructure **39**
Ready to Go? **52**

> **WHY PLAN?**
>
> My first VoIP experience occurred in the mid-1990s. I was using a dial-up Internet connection at 14.4 Kbps and the VocalTec Internet Phone softphone application. My system was an Intel 386 PC running Windows 95. I had a half-duplex sound card and a cheap desktop microphone.
>
> Imagine my surprise when my voice calls were spotty and slow. I couldn't talk at the same time as the other party and soon resorted to saying "Over" after each phrase (a throwback to my CB radio experience).
>
> It soon dawned on me that either Voice over IP was not ready for prime time or I was not ready for Internet phone. The reality was someplace in the middle. Without a fast modem and better sound card, I would never get decent voice quality. Without a headset microphone, my calls would be full of echoes.
>
> I shelved Internet Phone for a while and began watching (wistfully) the developments in business Voice over IP. I promised myself I would get back in when consumer VoIP worked better.
>
> I could have been using VoIP much sooner if I had planned better. If I had installed a faster modem, or if I had subscribed to an ISDN or Frame Relay Internet service, I would have had much better luck. If I had purchased a Pentium computer (just out), a full-duplex sound card, and a headset microphone, I would have had a much better phone experience. Of course, this would have added significantly to my telecommunications expenses, canceling any savings I hoped to have.
>
> Having an implementation plan would have exposed both outcomes. I would have known that I was not ready for VoIP, both because of cost and because of quality. As a result of my bad experience, I entered the consumer market much later than many of the early adopters, who have been enjoying VoIP for almost a decade.

Assessing Your Infrastructure

VoIP places certain demands on your home's Internet connection. If you have networking devices, your VoIP installation needs to coexist peacefully with them. You need to take into account devices such as firewalls, gateways, cable and DSL modems, and PCs, and also form a plan for integrating VoIP.

In this section, I look at the demands VoIP will place on your network and some likely installation points for your new devices.

Got network?

Many homes with broadband Internet use home gateway devices to connect their cable or DSL modem to one or more computers. If you have a laptop, you may have chosen a wireless gateway to allow you to wander about as you compute. Wireless or not, if you have an Internet gateway, you have a network.

A VoIP telephone adapter will need to find a home in your network infrastructure. Take a few moments to sketch your network to help you visualize the best place to plug in.

A NETWORK SKETCH

Your network sketch doesn't need to be anything fancy; a simple diagram on a sheet of paper is fine. Your main goal is to be able to visualize your system and to select proper equipment and locations for your phone system.

Use symbols to map out your devices. You can use the diagram I have included as a guide for symbols and formatting, or make up your own (**Figure 3.1**). You are the only one who needs to be able to understand your map.

FILLING IN VITAL STATISTICS

As you complete your drawing, fill in details such as Internet connection bandwidth and location of devices (**Figure 3.2**). You will use this information in your evaluation of your readiness for VoIP.

It is a good idea to test your bandwidth in addition to knowing what you are supposed to have. Almost all Internet connections perform at somewhat less than the speed advertised. You can test your bandwidth at a bandwidth site such as www.bandwidthplace.com or www.dslreports.com/stest.

Let's look at the phones

You might only have a single phone that you will be using with your service. If so, great! Meet me in the next section. If you would like to connect more than one phone to your Internet phone system, take a quick look at your current configuration.

Mapping out your phone system is also important to your planning effort (**Figure 3.3**). You should have a clear picture of how you plan to connect any existing phones you have to your new telephone adapter. As you map your system, note the location of each phone jack.

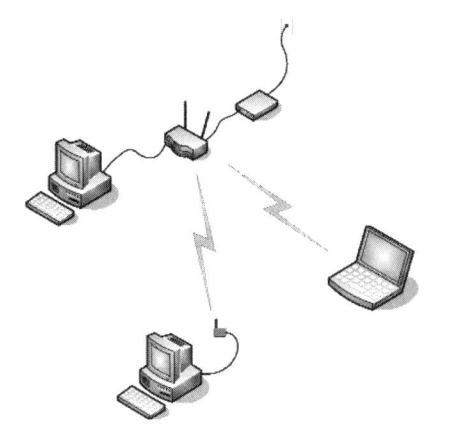

Assessing Your Infrastructure CHAPTER THREE 41

Figure 3.1 A basic network diagram showing the orientation of network devices

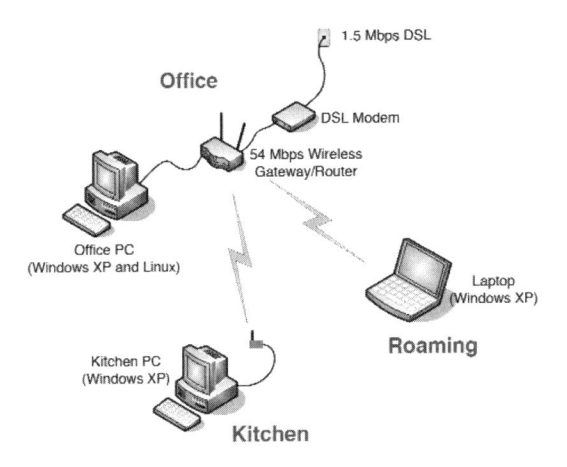

Figure 3.2 The network diagram with location and bandwidth information added

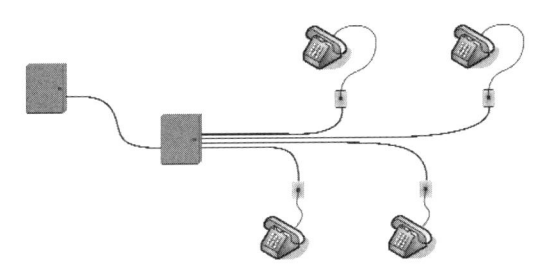

Figure 3.3 A basic diagram of a home's telephone distribution system

NIU (DEMARCATION POINT)

Phone companies connect to your home at a *demarcation point*, also called a *demarc* or *network interface unit (NIU)*. This device acts as a junction point for wires running from within your home to the telephone company's cables (**Figure 3.4**). When you install your telephone adapter, you may need to modify connections inside this device to distribute telephone signals throughout your home. We will discuss this process in more detail in Chapter 4. For now, just note the location of this device on your phone system map.

DISTRIBUTION

Your home's telephone cables originate in the demarcation point and proceed to jacks throughout your home. Inspect the demarcation point carefully to see how many cables run to the inside. Some installers run each cable individually out to the demarcation point; others use a distribution block inside the home to pass the signal to each individual jack (**Figure 3.5**). In Chapter 4, I discuss special steps to take if your cables terminate in the demarcation point.

ACCESS

If you live in an apartment building or townhome complex, you may not have direct access to the telephone company's demarcation point. If so, please note this on your drawing; it may affect the way you connect your phones to your telephone adapter.

Not having access to this connection point means you may not be able to disconnect the telephone company's cables. This can lead to stray voltages being sent from the telephone company into your system—a situation that has been known to damage telephone adapters. I discuss options for this situation in Chapter 4.

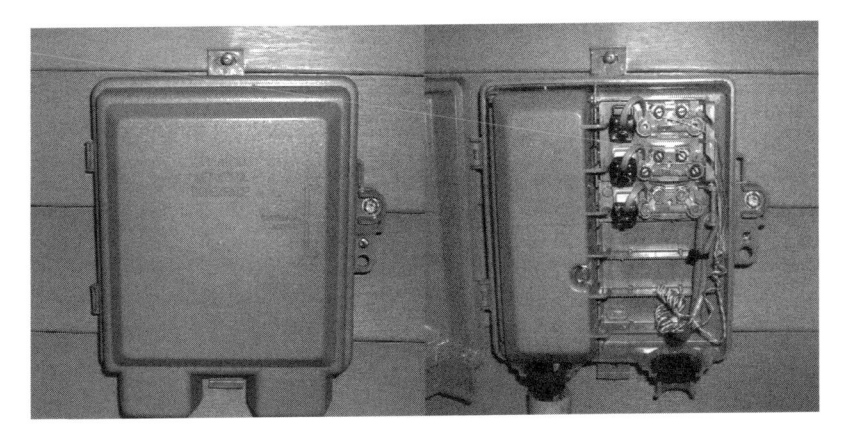

Assessing Your Infrastructure CHAPTER THREE 43

Figure 3.4 A telephone company's demarcation point or network interface unit (NIU)

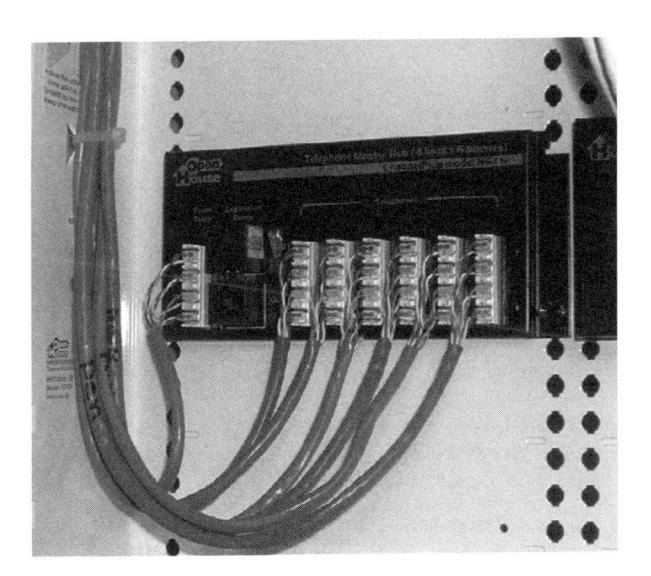

Figure 3.5 A telephone distribution panel in a home

Identify your challenges

After completing your drawings, you will assess your readiness for VoIP installation (**Figure 3.6**). Look for factors that may pose a challenge to your installation. Identify factors like bandwidth, telephone company interconnection, and device placement, and form a strategy to deal with these issues.

In this section, I examine these challenges and identify possible strategies for dealing with them.

BANDWIDTH

Bandwidth (or the lack thereof) is one of the leading contributors to poor voice quality. As I discussed in Chapter 1, each voice codec has different bandwidth requirements. Other factors that affect bandwidth use include the VoIP transport protocol, TCP/IP protocol overhead (the bandwidth used

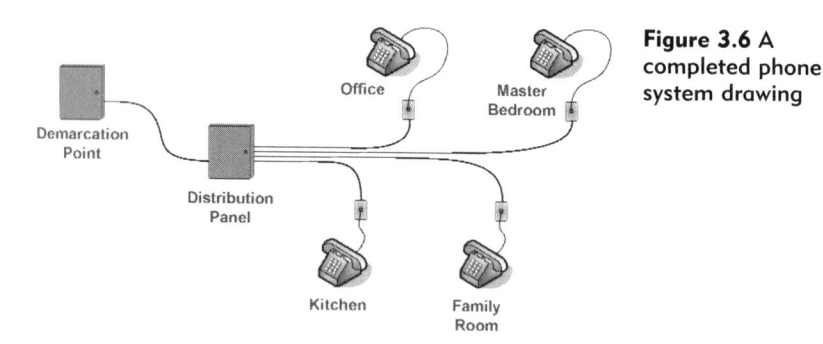

Figure 3.6 A completed phone system drawing

QUALITY OF SERVICE (QOS)

You will often see discussions of Quality of Service (QoS) in relation to VoIP calls. QoS is the ability of certain types of Internet traffic to take priority over others. This priority traffic will be given first access to available bandwidth. VoIP protocols do take precedence over most uses but can still be affected by sustained high-volume traffic of lower priority types. QoS prioritizes certain traffic but cannot hold off all other traffic indefinitely.

just to keep a connection alive), and Internet bandwidth used concurrently with voice calls.

Table 3.1 shows a breakdown of VoIP bandwidth minimums.

If you plan to use your Internet connection for other purposes while making voice calls, you should include an additional factor to account for that use. Moderate Web browsing will be unlikely to cause any problems in a 512 Kbps Internet connection, but heavy file downloading may significantly affect voice-call quality.

As you consider bandwidth, keep in mind that even advertised bandwidth fluctuates slightly during use. Most Internet access providers use a practice called *provisioning* to help them budget bandwidth allocation. They assume that most connections will not use the full advertised rate 100 percent of the time. They base their available bandwidth capabilities on a guess as to what percentage their customers will typically use. If they guess low, you will experience bandwidth restrictions, or *bottlenecks*. When this happens, you will receive somewhat less than your advertised bandwidth.

Table 3.1 VoIP Bandwidth Requirements

Codec	G.711	G.723	G.726	G.729
Used by codec	64 Kbps	5.3–6.3 Kbps	16–40 Kbps	6-8 Kbps
Transport (RTP)	20 Kbps	20 Kbps	20 Kbps	20 Kbps
TCP/IP overhead	6 Kbps	6 Kbps	6 Kbps	6 Kbps
Total	90 Kbps	32.3 Kbps	66 Kbps	34 Kbps

To see how often this happens, test your Internet bandwidth periodically. Sites like www.bandwidthplace.com offer free speed tests, and some sites offer specific testing for VoIP users (**Figure 3.7**). A Google search for "voip speed test" will reveal a list of suitable testing sites. Testing sites supported by specific VoIP vendors will indicate how many calls you can support concurrently when using their VoIP services.

There are a few ways to address bandwidth issues. If you are very interested in a specific VoIP provider, and bandwidth is an issue with its service, you might have no choice but to upgrade your Internet connection speed. Often, this is as simple as calling your Internet access provider and asking for an upgrade. Occasionally, upgrading might require additional or updated Internet connection devices to be installed in your home.

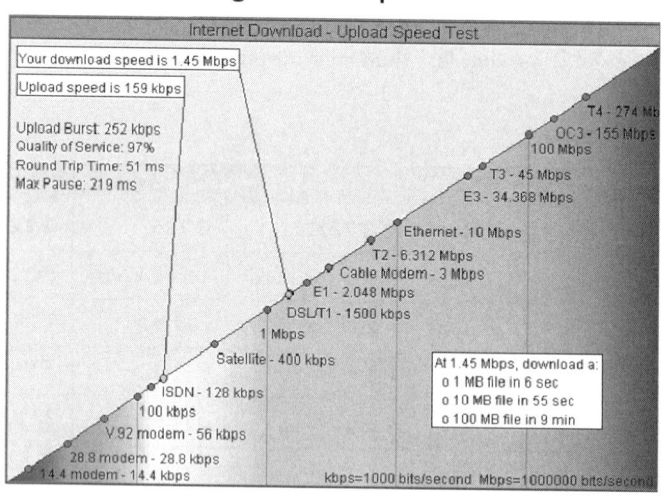

Figure 3.7 VoIP testing results displaying VoIP qualification scores

If you are not set on a specific VoIP provider, you might choose to use a provider that uses a lower-bandwidth codec. Some providers use G.711 as their sole supported codec; others allow you to choose among three or four codec options, depending on your needs. Often, these options are simplified to High, Medium, and Low in the provider's literature. A call to the provider's support department usually will get you the actual codec names.

If your bandwidth issue is caused by concurrent use of other Internet functions, such as Web browsing or e-mail, you might simply choose to avoid these activities while making calls. This is simpler when you are in total control of the system. If you are playing EverQuest in the office while your significant other is trying to make a call, this option might not work so well. EverQuest will take forever to update, and you might have to sleep on the couch.

> **SOME SOURCES OF BANDWIDTH ARE BETTER THAN OTHERS**
>
> You might be looking at the speed results of your satellite Internet connection and thinking, "Great! I have 400 Kbps. That should be plenty fast for VoIP."
>
> Not so fast.
>
> Certain types of Internet bandwidth are fine for uses such as Web browsing but do not work so well for VoIP use. Access methods such as satellite transmit your Internet traffic up into space and then down to a satellite uplink station. Then responses to your transmission are sent back up into the air and down to your dish. All this takes time, often measurable in seconds.
>
> Although this may be acceptable for Web browsing, delays of more than a second make conversation difficult. One person thinks it is okay to talk and begins talking, only to discover that the other party began talking first.
>
> When you are testing your bandwidth, look for statistics such as round-trip time (RTT). This is a measure of how long it will take for one speaker to know that the other is speaking. Anything less than 250 milliseconds should be fine.

LOSS OF DSL

If your bandwidth is supplied by a DSL Internet access service, and you truly want to "fire the phone company," you should be aware that most telephone companies will not provide DSL access without an active phone line. Some providers, such as Speakeasy.net, will connect DSL only but are not widely available yet.

If you stand to lose DSL service when you disconnect your telephone, you have a few options:

- Check with a competitive DSL provider for availability in your area. Providers like Speakeasy.net offer DSL on lines that they lease from the phone company. They don't care if you don't maintain phone service. In fact, they will be glad to offer you their own VoIP service to make calls over their DSL. Often, you will be offered a special price on a combination package of DSL and voice.

- Some local phone companies now offer DSL-only service. Inquire with your phone company to see whether this service is offered in your area.

- Don't forget the cable company. Cable Internet bandwidths are topping 7 Mbps these days. This is plenty fast for VoIP use, and VoIP speed-testing tools you might use will often report that you can maintain 7 to 10 concurrent calls at this bandwidth level.

NETWORK RECONFIGURATION

If you do not currently have a good place to insert your telephone adapter, you might have to reconfigure your network so that you can connect it. Consider the network shown in **Figure 3.8**. Some potential telephone adapter connection points are marked.

Until now, you might not have considered using a network at home. Your connections might look something like **Figure 3.9**.

If this is your situation, you'll need to find a way to get your telephone adapter connected. Purchasing a gateway (about $60) is often the best way to expand your connection options. You can choose either wired or wireless gateways.

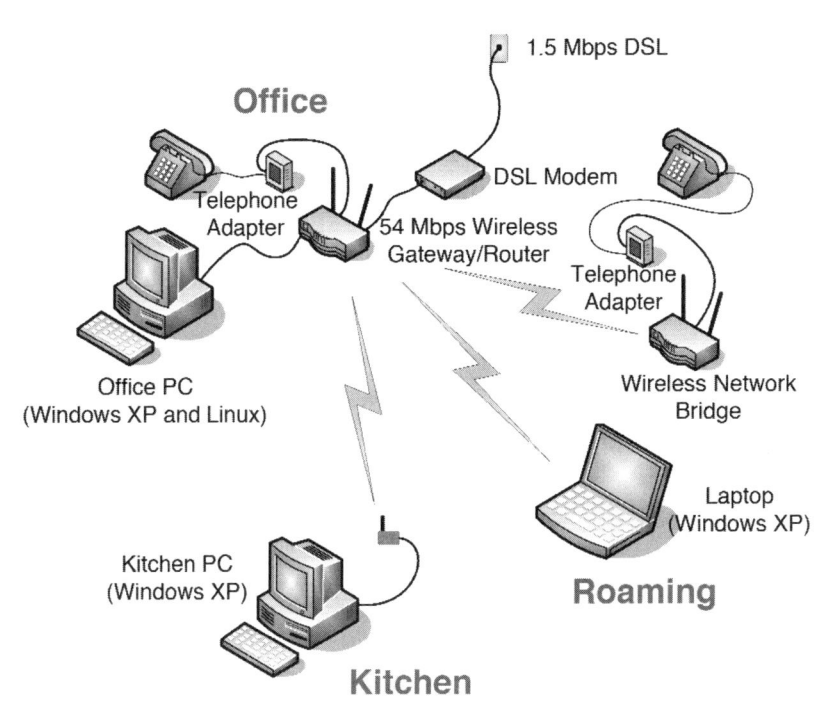

Assessing Your Infrastructure   CHAPTER THREE   49

Figure 3.8 Telephone adapter connected directly to gateway or on a wireless bridge

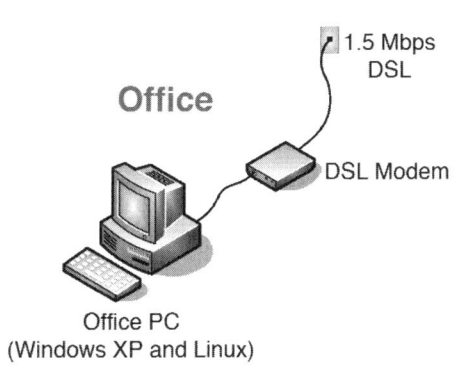

Figure 3.9 Internet access plan with no gateway device

Each will work as well as the other for providing access to connect your telephone adapter.

After installing a gateway, you can install your telephone adapter (**Figure 3.10**).

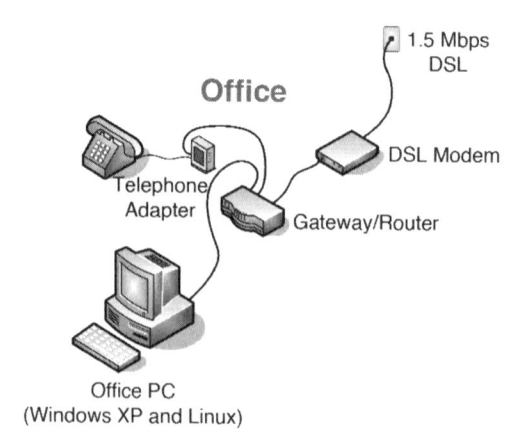

Figure 3.10 Your network reconfigured with an Internet gateway and telephone adapter

DEMARCATION CONCERNS

Your home telephone system is connected to the telephone company's systems at a demarcation point. Often, this point is located on the side of your home, but with townhomes, apartments, and condominiums, it may be in another part of the building. With apartments and condos, you may not even actually own the telephone line connecting your phones to the demarcation point. In these situations, you might have to find alternative means to distribute your telephone signals to the phones in your home.

Some installers use the demarcation point as a junction box for cable runs in your home. In this case, your phone cables are interconnected electrically at the demarcation point. You must take care when disconnecting the telephone company's cabling (covered in Chapter 4) to prevent disconnecting part of your phone system.

DISTRIBUTION CONCERNS

You might want to use VoIP for an inexpensive second line for business calls. Perhaps you would like to use your home's existing phone system to distribute the phone signal to other phones in your home (**Figure 3.11**). This requires the transmission of both the telephone company's signals and your Internet phone signals over the same cabling system. This is possible with a little careful configuration (covered in Chapter 4).

Telephone

Internet Phone

Figure 3.11 Telephone and Internet phone can be transmitted on the same cable.

WIRED GATEWAY VS. WIRELESS GATEWAY

Unless you are planning to use wireless network devices in your network, you can choose a gateway device that does not have this feature. If you are planning to use wireless devices such as laptop computers, you should purchase a wireless gateway.

You local computer store should have both types in stock. Ask an associate for assistance. Follow the included instructions to install the device in your network.

If you choose a wireless gateway, observe the security precautions recommended for wireless Internet connections. Activate Wired Equivalent Privacy (WEP) at minimum or, preferably, Wi-Fi Protected Access (WPA). These encryption mechanisms prevent external access to your network, keeping your data and communications private.

Ready to Go?

Most VoIP installations are relatively trouble free. The point of this chapter is not to frighten you into inaction, but to introduce some of the challenges you'll face when you actually replace a telephone system with VoIP.

In the next few chapters, you will proceed to install a VoIP system using the plans and challenges discussed here. You will discover that these challenges are easily surmountable and that you will have a stronger, more familiar telephone-style experience with your new system.

CHAPTER FOUR

Installing Your VoIP Equipment

Which came first: the VoIP hardware or the service activation? Some VoIP service providers need to have their equipment installed before you activate your service; others need to be activated before you attempt to connect. In this chapter and the next, I will discuss both, concentrating on hardware in this chapter and following up with service activation and testing in Chapter 5.

Whether you are going to use a telephone adapter, a combination Internet gateway and telephone adapter, or a softphone, you will want to use the guides in this chapter to ensure that your installation goes smoothly. Nothing is more frustrating than trying to isolate the cause of a voice-quality problem and not knowing whether the cause lies in the service or in your own wires.

By following the procedures in this chapter, you will give yourself some assurance that any problems that arise are not of your own making. If line issues do come up, you will be familiar with your installation and should be able to isolate the cause quickly.

IN THIS CHAPTER

Getting Your Network Ready **54**

Installing a Telephone Adapter **57**

Installing a Combination TA/Gateway **60**

Installing Internet Phone with Cable Systems **67**

Installing Softphone Accessories **68**

Distributing the Telephone Signal **69**

Summary **76**

Getting Your Network Ready

Without an Internet connection, your TA would make a pretty good paperweight. The cables kind of clutter your desktop, though, so you might want to leave them in the box.

In this section, I outline the things you need to do to get your network ready for VoIP communications. I sketch out a basic home office network and show you where your TA can be connected. I discuss settings you'll want to check out on your Internet gateway to ensure that you can connect to your VoIP service provider.

For simplicity and security, I recommend the use of an Internet gateway for connection to the Internet. However, if you do choose to connect your TA directly, without a gateway, I cover a few things you will need to do to get connected.

An Internet gateway device connects your home network to the Internet while protecting your computers from direct access by hackers. It includes features that filter out harmful traffic while allowing good traffic to reach your systems. Some gateways even offer the ability to restrict certain kinds of use by family members. These parental controls are recommended by child-safety advocates and law enforcement to protect children from online predators.

Internet gateway devices usually have one port that connects to your cable or DSL modem. This is called the *WAN (wide area network)* port. Traffic bound for this port must pass through your filters and controls before being allowed to reach computers on the inside.

Gateways also have one or more ports to which you connect computers on the internal network. These ports allow unrestricted access to other computers on the internal network to let you share files and printers or play network games. This activity occurs without any external indication of activity to tip off hackers. When an internal computer needs to access Internet resources, the gateway opens a connection to the Internet resource on behalf of the internal computer and acts as the go-between for the communications session.

Connecting your TA with an Internet gateway

When you connect your TA to an Internet gateway device, as shown in **Figure 4.1**, it will usually be assigned a network address by the gateway. When the TA attempts to connect to your VoIP service provider, it notifies the gateway that it wants to connect. The gateway opens a channel to the VoIP service provider to allow the TA to connect. This channel remains open as long as communication is taking place. Hackers see only the external address of your gateway, not the TA itself.

NOTE

Some gateways might not be configured to assign addresses automatically. If this is the case, you might have to manually assign your TA an address that will work on your network. This topic is covered in Chapter 6.

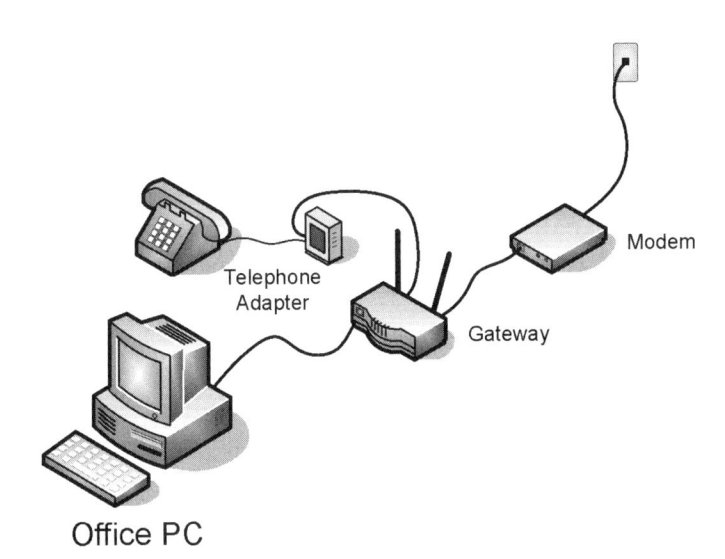

Figure 4.1 Your telephone adapter "all safe and sound" behind a gateway

TIP

If you plan to connect only a single computer to one of these devices, you can do without the switch depicted in Figure 4.2. A single computer can be connected directly to the TA itself.

Connecting without a gateway

Some TAs are designed to be placed outside your gateway (**Figure 4.2**). They connect between your network and the Internet. The D-Link DVG-1120 includes basic gateway functionality and can manage connections to internal computers on a second network port designed for this purpose.

If you connect a TA outside an Internet gateway, it essentially becomes the gateway to your network. It will manage addressing for one or more internal computers and also manage VoIP call processing. In many ways, this type of TA is very similar to a combination TA and gateway but offers somewhat less functionality when it comes to features such as firewalls and parental controls. If these features are very important to you, you might consider a full-featured TA/gateway combo device. I discuss the selection and installation of these devices later in this chapter, in "Installing a Combination TA/Gateway."

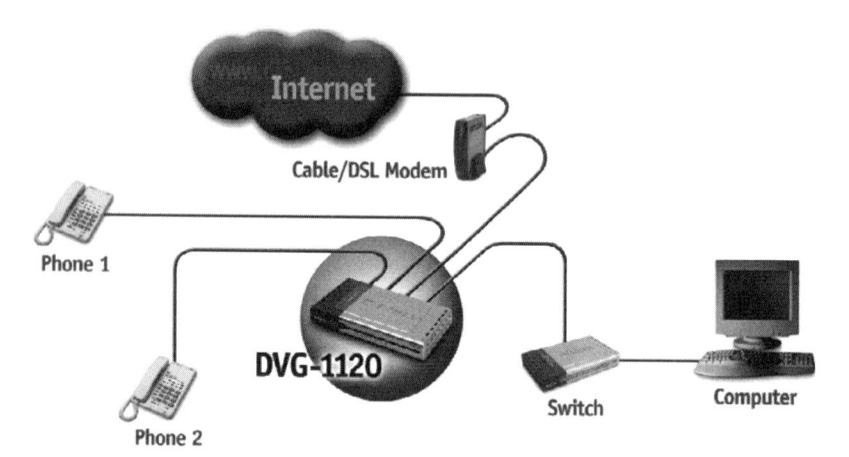

Figure 4.2 The D-Link DVG-1120 can be used as an Internet gateway device

Installing a Telephone Adapter

The majority of broadband Internet phone installations today use telephone adapters (TAs). These small devices convert the Internet bits and bytes to signals that a common, everyday telephone can understand (**Figure 4.3**). In addition, they convert your dialing tones to instructions that the VoIP provider uses to route your call.

Properly installing your TA will help ensure that you have a successful VoIP installation. Your TA will be able to locate your VoIP provider and properly insert itself into the provider's network. Your phones will work properly with your TA, and you can even configure your phone lines to distribute Internet phones throughout your home.

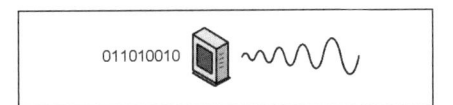

Figure 4.3 The telephone adapter converts digital Internet communications to analog audio signals.

Connecting your TA

Your TA should include a quick-start guide for connecting it to your network and telephones (**Figure 4.4**). You should read this guide carefully before beginning your installation. It will provide pictures to help you locate the proper ports for your connections, a simple step-by-step procedure for connecting, and a list of precautions to help you avoid problems.

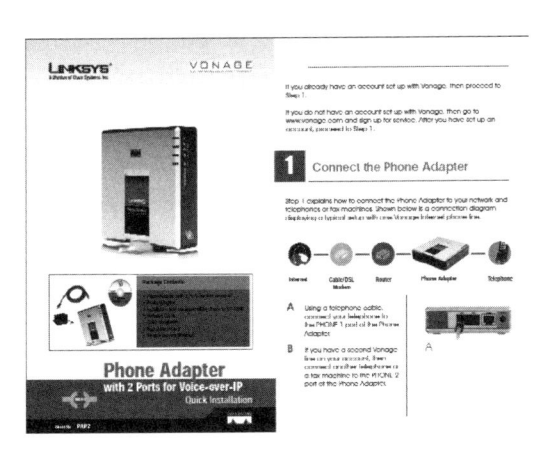

Figure 4.4 Quick-start guides are included with telephone adapters to help you set up your device quickly.

> **NOTE**
>
> In this section, I describe the installation process for a TA, from Internet connection to telephone handset connection. I also describe some of the possible configuration scenarios you may encounter when setting up your service. These instructions are, by necessity, somewhat generic. The wide variety of TAs now available makes a detailed model-specific guide impossible in the context of this book. What you will learn, however, are the general steps and gotchas to look for as you install your own device. Your device will include a setup guide that will assist you with specific installation steps for your TA that you can use along with what you learn here.

> **TIP**
>
> Often, you will be directed to complete your service activation before powering on your telephone adapter. This allows your VoIP service provider to have a connection prepared for your device on its end. If you are using a telephone adapter ordered directly from your VoIP service provider, it will be preactivated and can be powered on immediately. For more information on service activation, see Chapter 5.

> **NOTE**
>
> If your Internet gateway does not automatically assign an address to your TA, you may have to use your telephone handset to address the TA manually. Your TA has a voice-response menu that you can use to configure these settings. Look for instructions on this procedure in the user manual that comes with the device. Also, I discuss this scenario in Chapter 6.

INSTALLATION STEPS

The installation procedure for a TA device is quick. As you perform the installation, you typically take the following steps:

1. Generally, you connect your TA to your network and telephones before applying power to the device. This ensures that the device does not experience power surges or send voltage spikes to your other devices.

2. After connecting your TA, you apply power to the device. Observing the status lights will allow you to determine whether the device has successfully located its mother ship and established communications.

3. When your TA is communicating, you may perform additional steps to complete your configuration. You may dial configuration codes into your telephone or use your computer's Internet browser to access configuration menus.

CONNECTING YOUR PHONE

In addition to connecting a telephone directly to your TA, you might want to connect your TA to your home's telephone distribution system. I discuss this topic in depth later in this chapter, in "Distributing the Telephone Signal."

Checking your work

If everything proceeds according to plan, you should be hearing a dial tone from your TA. This tone indicates that the TA has established contact with your VoIP service provider and is ready to make calls. All status lights should be lit in accordance with the manufacturer's instructions.

If you do not hear a dial tone, or if you hear a busy signal, your TA might not be finding the VoIP service provider. You might have to troubleshoot settings or repeat a portion of the configuration process to get it working properly.

All appropriate status lights should be lit. If not, troubleshoot the connection that does not show a light. Network issues such as a missing address will prevent the network status light from lighting. You can troubleshoot address settings by using the steps I outline in Chapter 6. If status lights do not appear for VoIP ports, you might have to contact your VoIP service provider to see whether there are configuration problems with your account.

Safety concerns

You might wonder how there can be anything dangerous about VoIP communications. Aside from what is being said over the telephone, Internet phone communications are very safe. Just keep a few things in mind when dealing with telephone circuits.

RING VOLTAGES

To make your telephone ring, your local phone company puts a ring voltage on your phone line. The voltage is usually between 65 and 90 volts and can shock you if you happen to be touching an exposed wire when the ring comes through.

Your TA can generate the same voltages. Use caution when handling phone wires and plugs to avoid learning any new dance steps.

HEAT

Your TA generates a fair amount of heat when it's in use. Avoid placing it under a hat or a big fluffy pillow. It should be placed in a position where it can get good airflow in the bottom and out the top so that heat can be removed by natural convection. See a physicist for more details.

> **TIP**
>
> Most quick-start guides assume certain network conditions. It is common to assume, for example, that the TA installation will be behind a gateway that automatically assigns IP addresses. Deviations from this basic environment will require some changes in your installation plan. Reading this book and the documentation included with your TA should equip you with the information you need to manage this process.

Installing a Combination TA/Gateway

Telephone adapters with built-in Internet gateway capabilities give you a great opportunity to integrate network and phone services in your home. With a single device, you can distribute Internet access to multiple computers in your home while providing Internet phone to as many as two callers at once (**Figure 4.5**).

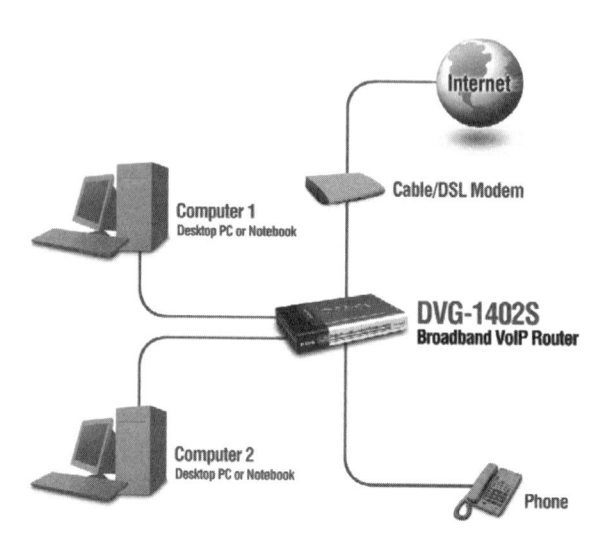

Figure 4.5 The D-Link DVG-1402S VoIP Router being used as an Internet gateway

This increased functionality does cost a bit more than a simple TA, but the extra cost is worth it if you don't already own an Internet gateway device. Having Internet access combined with VoIP functionality also makes it simpler to configure Internet phone service. As TA configuration steps are completed, the setup utility automatically ensures that the gateway is configured to allow Internet phone traffic to pass between the TA portion of the device and the Internet. This eliminates configuration issues that might arise with physically separate TA devices.

In addition to the type of gateway shown above, you can purchase TA/gateways that add wireless networking functionality to the mix (**Figure 4.6**). Devices like Linksys' WRT54GP2 do it all. They not only manage VoIP calling, but also network both wired and wireless computers.

Figure 4.6 The WRT54GP2 from Linksys offers wireless networking capability in addition to TA and gateway capabilities.

NOTE

Be sure to activate your VoIP service before installing your router. This step will ensure that the provider's systems are listening for it when it comes online.

Connecting your gateway

A TA/gateway combination is first and foremost an Internet gateway. It is often an existing Internet gateway design that has had VoIP functionality incorporated. Let's look at how you can use this device to network your home.

BUILDING A HOME NETWORK

You should consider a gateway if you have more than one computer that accesses the Internet. The gateway acts as the central network connection point. Each computer connects to the gateway, either with a cable or wirelessly via wireless Ethernet technology. Each computer has the ability to share files and communicate with any other computer on the network. You can also configure your computers to share devices such as printers and to support multiplayer network games.

Installing a gateway usually requires the following steps:

1. Connect the gateway device to your broadband (cable or DSL) modem.
2. Connect any computers that will be using your Internet connection to the gateway device.
3. Power on the gateway device.
4. Connect to the gateway with your computer's Internet browser (the address will be supplied in your setup guide).

5. Configure gateway connection settings to activate Internet access and set up internal network support.

6. Test Internet access from all connected computers.

You might connect phones at this point, or you might wait until you are sure that you have a stable Internet connection using the gateway.

CONFIGURING YOUR INTERNET SETTINGS

Depending on the specifics of your broadband connection, you may have to configure Internet access settings for your gateway. Often, the modem will manage the process of connecting to the Internet; all that is required is to connect the gateway. The gateway receives an address from the modem and goes right to work. At other times, you might have to configure your gateway to supply a user name and password so you can connect (**Figure 4.7**). Which method you employ depends on your Internet access provider. Its technical staff should be able to guide you quickly through this setup process.

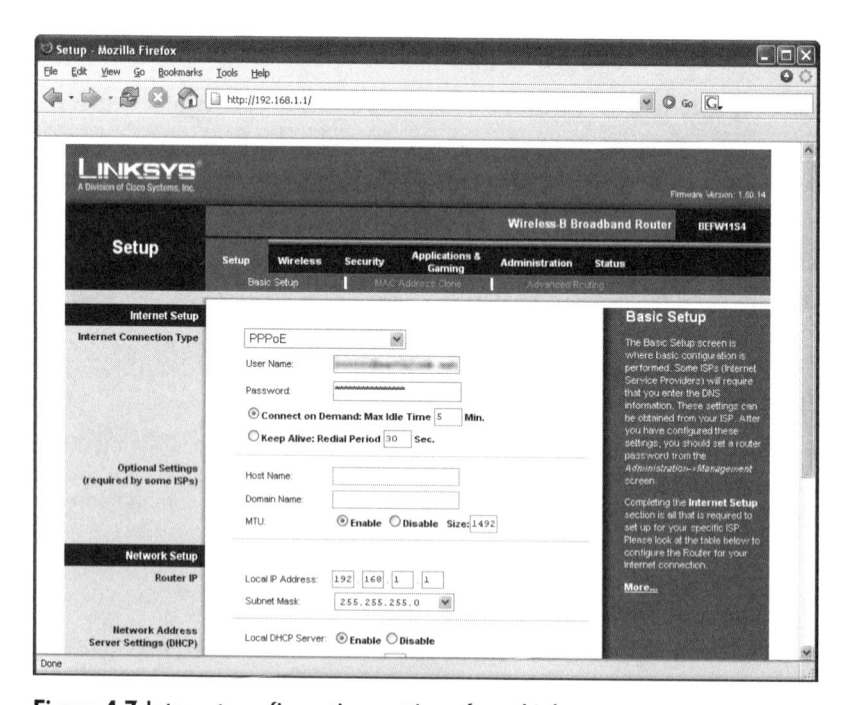

Figure 4.7 Internet configuration settings for a Linksys gateway

Your gateway should have a device status page that allows you to view the status of your Internet connection (**Figure 4.8**). You can use this page to verify that your configuration settings have been successful.

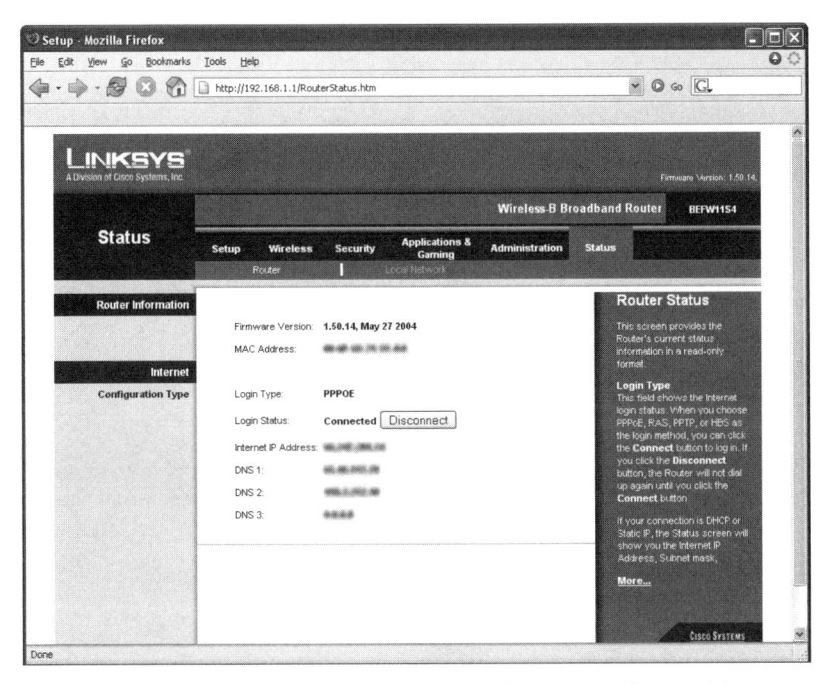

Figure 4.8 Viewing Internet connection status (Internet addresses blurred to protect the innocent)

> **TIP**
>
> Don't let the helpful young person with only your Internet well-being at heart talk you into buying more expensive Category 6 cables. It will be many years before Internet connections need a cable of this rating. (By then, we will probably be wearing high collars and using subspace radios anyway.) Category 5 cables are plenty good for home use and cost less than half what the gold-plated-contact, low-oxide, high-twist, matched-pair, <insert new, impressive-sounding marketing angle here> Cat6 cables run.

CONNECTING NETWORK CLIENT COMPUTERS

You will connect computers to your gateway with cables. Often, the cables come with the gateway; you can purchase others where you bought your gateway.

When you connect your computer, watch the status lights on your gateway. As you plug each cable in and power on the computer, you should see a status light come on for the appropriate port on the gateway. This is an indication that the connection is good. If you do not see a light, check your connections.

> **NOTE**
>
> Contrary to popular belief that this name stands for **P**acket **IN**ternet **G**roper, ping was designed by a gentleman who just needed a way to test a connection one night at Berkeley. He thought of submarine movies and the "ping" they used to locate other ships on sonar. He named this utility ping in honor of those old movies.

Most modern computer operating systems automatically detect the environment they are started in and configure the appropriate network settings. You should be able to open a browser and get right online.

Testing Internet connectivity

Beside launching your browser and visiting Web sites, you can use other tools to check your Internet connections.

PING

The most commonly used Internet troubleshooting tool is ping (**Figure 4.9**). This utility works by sending a small packet of data to a designated address on a network. If the host is up, it replies with another packet. This return packet validates the connection.

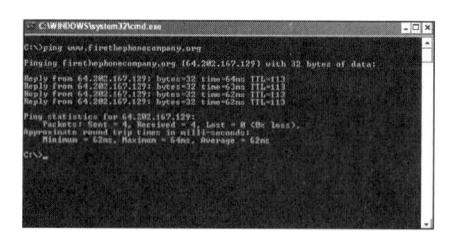

Figure 4.9 Using ping to test a connection to the Internet

To use ping to test your connections, you ping several addresses, beginning with yours and moving out to remote Internet addresses.

A typical ping test might employ the following steps:

1. Ping your own computer's loopback testing address. This command looks like this:

    ```
    C:\ping localhost
    ```

    A successful loopback ping verifies that your Internet protocols are working.

2. Next, ping your own IP address. You can find this address by using the `ipconfig` command:

    `C:\ipconfig`

    `ipconfig` will report your address. Then you can use it with ping to verify that your computer's network interface is alive:

    `C:\ping <your own address>`

3. Ping your gateway, which tests your ability to communicate on your local network.

4. Ping an Internet address, which tests your computer's ability to locate the remote system's address and communicate with it.

PATHPING

Pathping is a tool that tests connectivity and also connection quality (**Figure 4.10**). It functions by sending 100 test packets to a destination host and counting the number it receives in return. If Pathping receives 100 packets in return, your connection is classified as 100%.

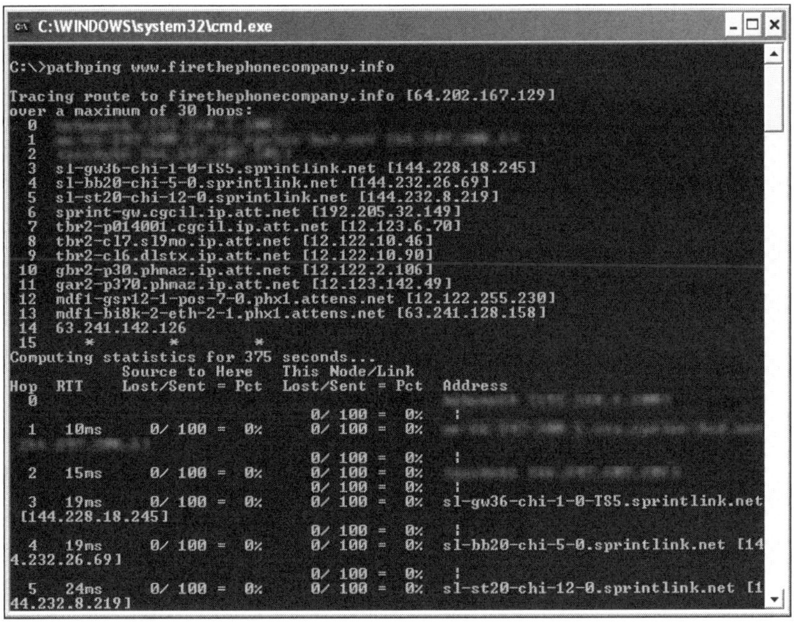

Figure 4.10 Pathping testing connection quality to a remote site

> **TIP**
>
> You can reverse the order of these steps if you have a high degree of certainty that your local settings are correct. This could help you locate the problem area more quickly.

> **NOTE**
>
> Pathping is not available on all systems. Windows systems before Windows 2000 do not include this utility.

This test can give you an idea of where there might be problems between your system and a remote site. It qualifies each successive stage in the path to the site, showing you where packets are getting dropped.

Pathping is used like this:

```
C:\pathping <remote address>
```

Configuring your telephone settings

After Internet connectivity is established, don't be surprised if your TA goes out and finds its service. For this reason, be sure to visit your VoIP provider's activation page to activate your router before installing your router.

Most routers will have the TA configuration locked down if they are intended for a specific service provider. To manage these settings, you'll need to work with your provider's technical support staff.

Manual addressing issues do not exist with this configuration, because the router manages all connection requirements for the TA.

Connecting your phone

In addition to connecting a telephone directly to your TA, you might want to connect your TA to your home's telephone distribution system. I discuss this topic in depth later in this chapter, in "Distributing the Telephone Signal."

Checking your work

If everything proceeds according to plan, you should be hearing a dial tone from your TA. This tone indicates that the TA has established contact with your VoIP service provider and is ready to make calls. All status lights should be lit in accordance with the manufacturer's instructions.

If you do not hear a dial tone, or if you hear a busy signal, your TA might not be finding the VoIP service provider. You might have to troubleshoot settings or repeat a portion of the configuration process to get it working properly.

All appropriate status lights should be lit. If not, troubleshoot the connection that does not show a light. If status lights do not appear for VoIP ports, you might have to contact your VoIP service provider to see whether there are configuration problems with your account.

Safety concerns

Earlier in this chapter, I discuss safety precautions to be aware of (see "Ring voltages" and "Heat").

Installing Internet Phone with Cable Systems

Most cable providers that offer digital phone services insist on installing the equipment themselves. They do not necessarily use Voice over IP technology at the point where you connect to their networks. The cable company usually connects its own network interface device (NIU) on an exterior wall of your home, and telephone lines will be run into the home from there. As with installation by a telephone company, you can access a portion of the NIU to connect additional phones to your system.

Getting started with digital phone services

Most cable operators will install your service for you. This is not only a good revenue stream for those companies, but also ensures that the installation is done without significant problems. If your cable operator offers VoIP services instead of a proprietary digital phone service, or if it offers no services at all beyond Internet access, you can use the procedures outlined in the preceding sections for installing TAs and TA/gateway combinations. In this scenario, you will be using the cable operator only for Internet access; all VoIP functionality will come from your selected VoIP provider.

TIP

VoIP is also an alternative to digital phones. If you are not impressed by your cable operator's offerings, just sign up with a VoIP service provider.

Managing digital phone distribution

The telephone cables in your home run either to a distribution panel inside the home or out to the telephone company's demarcation point. How you distribute digital phone service will depend on where the junctions are made.

JUNCTIONS IN THE NIU

If all your telephone cables run to the demarcation point, you can have them moved to the NIU. By connecting them together there, you ensure distribution throughout your home.

DISTRIBUTION PANEL

Some phone system installations run a single cable to a distribution panel inside the home. This panel then distributes the signal to all the phone cables for the home.

If your home is wired in this manner, you just need to get a phone cable to the distribution panel from the NIU. You'll patch it into the distribution panel in place of the cable coming in from the telephone company's demarcation point. You can find details on this process in the upcoming "Distributing the Telephone Signal" section.

Installing Softphone Accessories

Even softphones use hardware sometimes. In this section, I quickly cover the installation of USB handsets and computer headsets for use with softphone-based Internet phone services.

USB handset installation

USB handsets typically require little configuration. Your handset will be provided with drivers that enable you to use it to control the features of your softphone. Be sure to read the installation instructions carefully. Some manufacturers have you install the software and driver before plugging in your handset; others require you to insert the driver disk only when prompted by your computer.

A typical installation scenario looks like this:

1. Connect your USB handset to your computer.
2. Insert the software and driver disk when prompted to install drivers and software.
3. Follow the included configuration instructions to enable the handset to operate your softphone.

> **NOTE**
>
> Some handsets provide less than full functionality with certain operating systems. Read your handset's sales literature to make sure it will provide adequate functionality with your system.

Headphone installation

Installing a headphone is usually no more difficult than finding the proper jacks on the back of your computer. Your softphone software may offer an audio tuning feature that lets you set microphone and headphone levels for good communications (**Figure 4.11**).

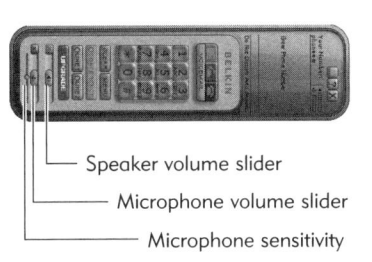

Figure 4.11 Audio settings in Belkin's callEverywhere softphone

- Speaker volume slider
- Microphone volume slider
- Microphone sensitivity

Distributing the Telephone Signal

So far, I have discussed the installation of your VoIP connection equipment to the Internet and to one telephone. Now it is time to share your new toys with the rest of the family.

In this section, I discuss ways to use your existing telephone distribution system to get Internet phone in other parts of the home. I also show you ways to distribute Internet phone in cases where you do not have access to the telephone company demarcation point or have no existing distribution system.

> **TIP**
>
> Place a small tag or sign in the demarcation point, warning telephone-company employees about your private system. It is possible that they may inadvertently reconnect the interface plug if they happen to be working in the box and see it unplugged. A simple "Private network—do not reconnect" should be sufficient.

First things first

Before you connect your VoIP devices to your home's telephone jacks, you'll want to do a few things. Among these are disconnecting the telephone company's lines from your demarcation point (to prevent damage to your equipment) and collecting the proper cables and connectors.

DISCONNECTING THE DEMARC

Even when the telephone company has disconnected your telephone lines, there is still the possibility that it may apply testing voltages to your wires from time to time. These voltages can cause problems with your VoIP devices. It is a good idea to disconnect the telephone company's cables at the demarcation point (**Figure 4.12**). Unplugging the telephone-company interface in the demarcation point ensures that there will be no stray voltages on your system.

GETTING THE RIGHT CABLES AND CONNECTORS

When connecting your TA to your home phones, you will need some standard telephone line cords, which you can purchase at your local electronics or hardware store. Ask for RJ-11 telephone line cords (**Figure 4.13**). These are four-wire cords that have the ability to carry up to two phone lines.

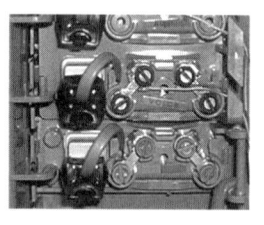

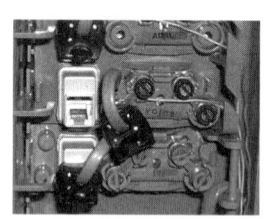

Figure 4.12 Disconnecting the phone-company cables in the demarcation point

Figure 4.13 An RJ-11 modular line cord

While you are there, ask whether the store has anything like the Allen Tel AT173 modular adapter (**Figure 4.14**). This device allows single phone devices to be connected to either of the two lines in a standard four-wire phone jack. You will use this adapter to manage two-line and split-line configurations, which I discuss later in this chapter.

> **TIP**
>
> Google "Allen Tel AT173" to find online retailers that sell this handy device.

Figure 4.14 The Allen Tel AT173 two-line modular adapter can connect phones to two different lines in one jack.

Connecting your TA to the distribution system

When the telephone company cables are disconnected, and you have all the proper cables and connectors, you can get started with your connections. There are a few scenarios to consider as you connect your phones:

- VoIP as a single line
- Two-line VoIP service
- VoIP as a second line with an existing telephone-company line

> **WHY DON'T ALL MY PHONE JACKS WORK?**
>
> When you connect to your phone system, you might notice that some jacks do not seem to work. This can happen when the demarcation point is also used as the distribution point. One or more of the cables leading into your home might not be connected.
>
> At the demarcation point, simply connect these disconnected wires to the same screws the other wires are using. Connect each color to the screw that has the same-color wires connected to it. Be careful not to reconnect the telephone company's wires.
>
> With all wires interconnected, you should have a dial tone at all jacks.

> **NOTE**
>
> Be sure to post a warning in the demarcation point to telephone-company personnel. If they come along and reconnect Line 2, your TA could fry.

CONNECTING AS A SINGLE-LINE SERVICE

The most common service type for those who plan to fire the phone company is a single-line VoIP service. In this scenario, you simply connect your TA to an available wall jack and use your home phones normally (**Figure 4.15**).

CONNECTING AS A TWO-LINE SERVICE

If you plan to use two VoIP lines, you can use the modular adapter plug discussed in "Getting the right cables and connectors" earlier in this chapter. When you connect this plug to your wall jack, you can plug Line 1 from your TA into the L1 port and Line 2 from the TA into the L2 port (**Figure 4.16**).

This arrangement places each line on a separate pair of wires in the jack. Then you can use adapters at other wall jacks to access the line you would like to use in that particular room. You can even directly connect a two-line phone to any jack or to the L1&L2 port on the adapter for access to both lines (**Figure 4.17**).

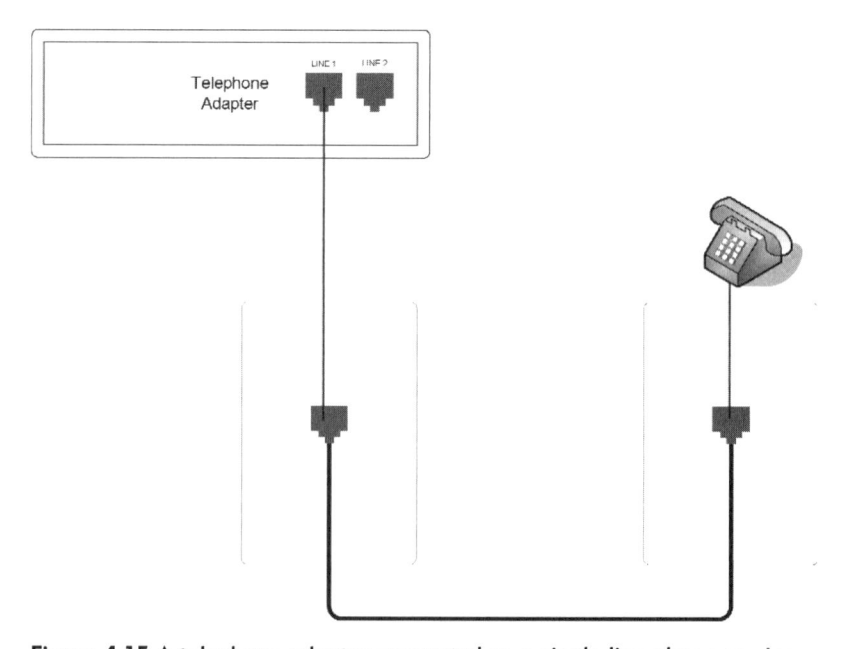

Figure 4.15 A telephone adapter connected as a single-line phone service

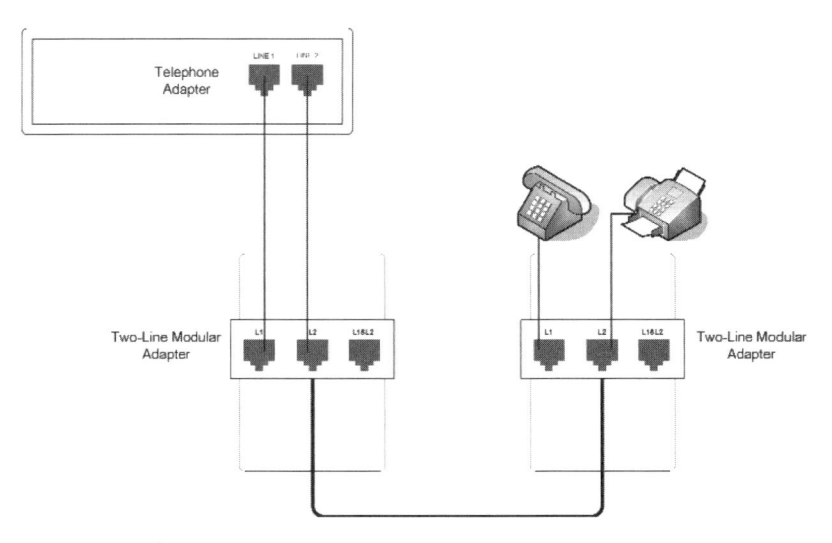

Distributing the Telephone Signal   CHAPTER FOUR   73

Figure 4.16 Connecting two VoIP lines to your home's phone system

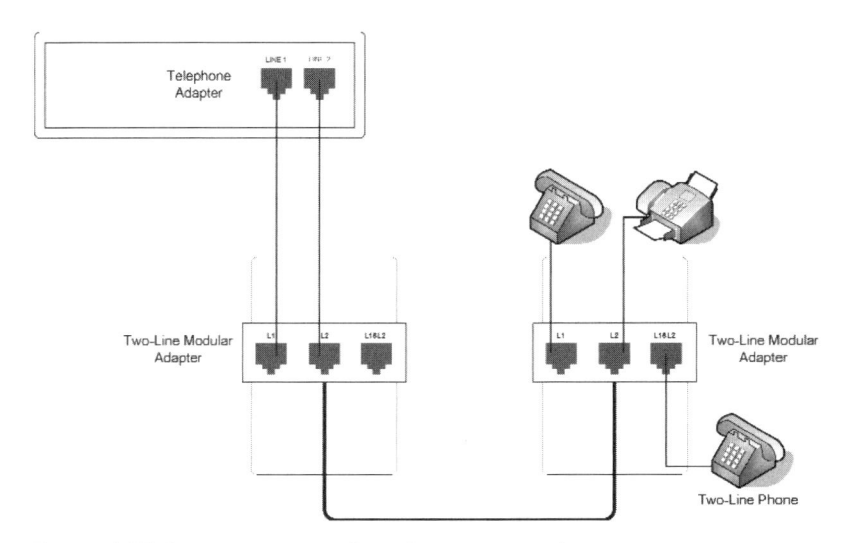

Figure 4.17 Connecting a two-line phone to your phone system

CONNECTING AS A SECOND LINE IN A TWO-LINE SERVICE

If you plan to keep one voice line from the telephone company, you can still get Internet phone in every room as a second line option. Accomplishing this requires careful configuration in the demarcation point. You will leave the telephone company's connector in place for Line 1 but remove the connector for Line 2, opening that line for connection to your TA (**Figure 4.18**).

Using the two-line modular adapter, connect your TA to the L2 port. Use additional adapters in other rooms to select the line you want to use. You will find the telephone-company line on L1 and your Internet phone on L2. You can also connect two-line phones directly into any jack for access to both lines (**Figure 4.19**).

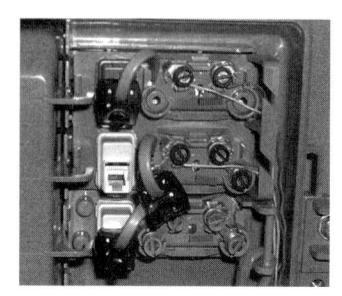

Figure 4.18 Leaving Line 1 connected at the demarcation point while disconnecting Line 2

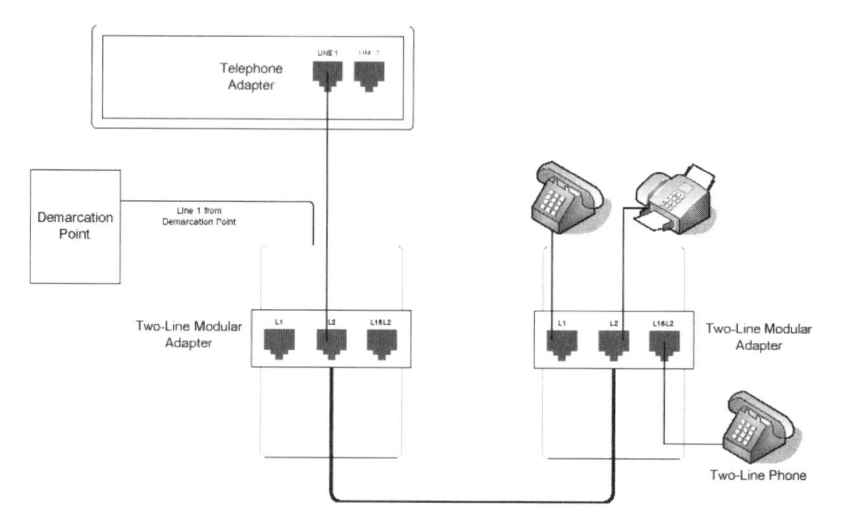

Figure 4.19 Connecting two-line phones to your shared system

Distributing telephone service without wires

If all this demarcation-point stuff is just too much, or if you do not have access to the demarcation point for your home, you might consider using cordless phones to access your Internet phone service.

CORDLESS PHONE OPTIONS

A simple cordless phone will allow you to roam about the place while you talk. For many homes, a single phone will be adequate. However, if you have a family, especially one with teens, you probably will opt for something like the Panasonic KX-TG2770S phone system (**Figure 4.20**).

This two-line phone system can access both lines concurrently and supports as many as eight handsets. This allows you to place handsets where they are easy to reach—all without opening a panel, jack, or faceplate!

Figure 4.20 The Panasonic KX-TG2770S two-line cordless phone system supports up to eight phones on two lines.

CONNECTING TWO-LINE CORDLESS PHONES TO YOUR TA

Remember the Allen Tel AT173 two-line modular adapter? Well, you guessed it: It has one more role to play. When you connect one VoIP line to L1 and another to L2, you can connect your two-line cordless base station to the L1&L2 plug for two-line access (**Figure 4.21**).

> **NOTE**
>
> For this use, do not connect the adapter to a wall jack; this could expose your equipment to telephone-company voltages. Instead, use the adapter with only the line cords plugged in; it has all the necessary circuitry to combine the two single lines into one two-line jack for your cordless phone.

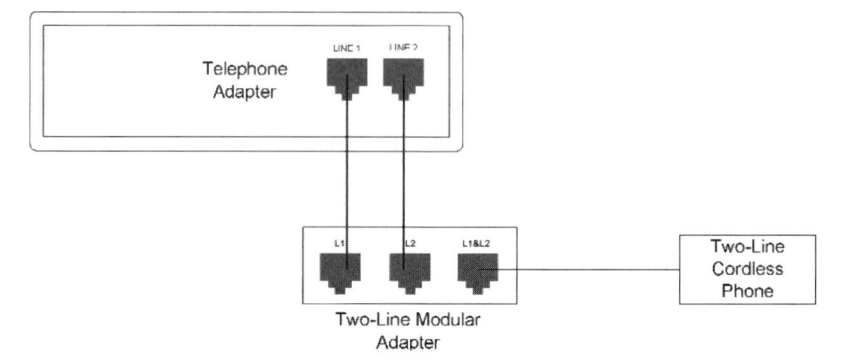

Figure 4.21 Using the Allen Tel AT173 to connect a two-line cordless phone

Summary

Installing VoIP equipment for basic functionality is not very difficult. As you have seen in the excerpts from quick-start guides, very few steps are involved. When you feel confident enough to tackle distribution issues, read this chapter again to make sure that you have everything you need.

By using what you have learned in this chapter, you should find it relatively simple to provide an excellent communication system for your home for the cost of a few adapters and cords.

CHAPTER FIVE

Setting Up Your Service

Subscribing to an Internet phone service and setting up the hardware are a sort of "chicken and egg" conundrum. Often, you will be doing both at once, so it may seem counterintuitive to split them into separate chapters. It is easier to understand the entire process, however, by splitting it into smaller pieces. After you have read both chapters, you will be able to reassemble the parts into a better understanding of the entire process. Then, when you install your own service, it will be simpler to understand what is going on.

In this chapter, I show you the options to consider as you turn on your service and the steps to take after installation to test and troubleshoot your new phone system.

> **IN THIS CHAPTER**
> Choosing a Purchase Option **78**
> Activating Your Service **80**
> Postactivation Setup **83**
> Installing Softphone-Only Services **97**
> Testing Your Internet Phone **100**
> Bringing It All Together **103**

> **NOTE**
>
> Most of the examples in this chapter depict the Vonage broadband phone service. This does not imply any particular preference on the author's part; the examples are intended to show configuration and management of a service consistently from start to finish. These procedures are common to all broadband phone services, although the screens or procedures may vary. For exact procedures for your chosen service, please refer to your provider's instructions.

Choosing a Purchase Option

I hinted in earlier chapters that *where* you purchase your Internet phone equipment will make a difference in how it is installed. The VoIP provider's communications network needs to know what to do with each telephone adapter (TA) that connects across the Internet. If your TA has not been registered with your provider, the provider's networks will not recognize it.

The process of registering your TA with the provider's network is called *activation*. In this section, I describe the basics of how activation works and how to perform activation for TAs purchased in a retail store.

Retail purchase and activation

When you buy a boxed Internet phone kit in the store, you receive the TA, some cables, and a quick-start guide (**Figure 5.1**). The TA will be ready to use, but you will need to make your VoIP provider's network aware that you exist before attempting to connect.

Before activation, the network would turn a deaf ear to your TA. During the activation process, you provide the TA's unique address to the provider's network, which causes the network to begin listening for your TA's call. Now when you attempt to connect, the network knows what to do with your device and how to integrate it with the range of features provided by your Internet phone company.

Internet purchase and activation

If you sign up for service online or over the phone, your VoIP provider will enter the address of a TA into its system before shipping it to you. When you receive the TA, it will be ready to go. In this case, you'll just connect it to the Internet and begin using it.

Figure 5.1 A package-contents list for the Linksys PAP2 telephone adapter

Activating Your Service

The process of activating an Internet phone service is fairly straightforward. If you have ever made an online or telephone purchase, you already know everything you need to know to activate your VoIP service.

A typical activation

Let's begin by assuming that you have purchased an Internet phone kit in the store. This is a common scenario for those who prefer to see and hold a device before buying it. It is also very economical, as the device is often free after rebates.

PURCHASE

When you select a TA in the store, you will make a few choices. You'll decide whether you want a simple TA or an Internet gateway that includes VoIP functionality. You might also make your final choice among competing VoIP services.

If you have been reading right along to this point, you should be prepared to make this decision. If you still have questions, however, don't make your decision in the store. Spend a little more time reading and researching service plans before going back to the store. The guys and gals in the store are helpful inasmuch as they are there to help you buy something. Whether the something you buy is the best choice for you is another topic entirely!

ACTIVATING YOUR TA

When you get home, you'll unpack your new TA. Prominently placed in the box will be a poster or booklet describing the setup process (**Figure 5.2**). As you read the instructions, you will see that a call or Internet visit to your provider is required to establish service. This contact registers your device with the service provider's network and registers your bank card with its subscription system.

Activating Your Service   CHAPTER FIVE   **81**

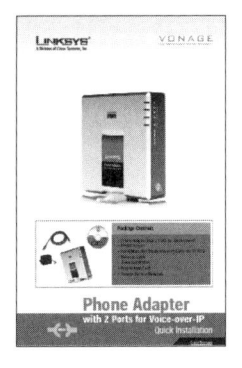

Figure 5.2 The Linksys quick-start guide for the PAP2 telephone adapter

Once again, if you have any questions about the best subscription option for you, back away, and do a little more research. Don't be distracted by the sexy front-page graphics and offers. Work out the minutes you are likely to use and what a lesser plan would cost, even with overages. You might be surprised to find that the "unlimited" plan is not the best deal.

During registration, you will be asked to enter the 12-digit MAC address located on the TA device (see the sidebar in this section). This number also frequently appears on the product packaging to enable the provider to activate kits without opening the box (**Figure 5.3**). Look for the bar-code sticker saying something like MAC ID: or MAC:. Enter the entire code, including zeros, in the registration screen.

When you complete the registration process, your setup guide will direct you through the completion of your installation.

Figure 5.3 Locating the MAC address on your product packaging

> **NOTE**
>
> If you purchased a TA that is already activated, you will begin here.

ESTABLISHING COMMUNICATIONS

After registering your TA, you will proceed to power on the device to establish communications.

After powering on the device, watch the status lights. The lights will blink as the power-up sequence continues; eventually, they will reach a state where they will be on most of the time, with only intermittent flickering as communications between the TA and the VoIP provider's systems take place. When this state has been reached (usually, within a minute), you are ready to make your first call.

Your first call

If you are like me, you are ready to make your first call and have to think for a minute about who to call first! You are proud of having set up this service but don't want to embarrass yourself by calling someone you know and having the call go badly.

My advice? Call a bank or some organization with a phone tree. This will allow you to listen to call quality and use touch tones to activate menu options. If the phone tree can make out the touch tones, chances are that your friends and family will hear you just fine. Now hang up and call someone to brag about your new phone service.

> **WHAT IS A MAC ADDRESS?**
>
> A *M*edia *A*ccess *C*ontrol address is a unique hexadecimal (powers of 16) number that identifies a network device on a network. MAC addresses are constructed by combining a manufacturer's code with a unique sequence of numbers assigned by the manufacturer.
>
> When your TA communicates with your VoIP provider's systems, the provider recognizes this address as the one you entered in the registration screen. For this reason, it is very important that you make sure you entered this sequence in your screen correctly. If you entered this address incorrectly, it will take a call to the VoIP provider's technical support staff to correct the problem.

Postactivation Setup

Although your Internet phone service will be functional following activation, you have a few important features to activate before you can relax. Foremost among these features is 911. If your provider supports 911 services, you'll need to register your address with its system. Registering your address enables your provider to locate the *public safety answering point (PSAP)* for 911 calls in your area. Sometimes, this setup is done as part of basic activation, but often, it is an additional step you must perform separately. Do not let this slip your mind. It will be too late to activate it when you really need it.

911 activation

The process of activation is actually fairly simple. You complete a form on your provider's Web site, and the provider configures your line. Let's take a look at the process.

REGISTERING YOUR LINE

When you register your 911 location, you need to provide the street address where your phone service is connected (**Figure 5.4**, next page). Your VoIP provider will use this information to locate the PSAP responsible for your area. This will be an actual emergency dispatch center. It is very important that you test your 911 service after activation to be sure your 911 access has been properly assigned.

TESTING YOUR 911 SERVICE

There have been several reported instances in which a customer did not activate his 911 service and ran into trouble when calling during an actual emergency. Others have set up 911 only to find that it was not routed properly during an actual emergency. For this reason, it is important not only to register your 911 location, but also to test the service after you have been notified that it is ready to use.

84 CHAPTER FIVE Setting Up Your Service

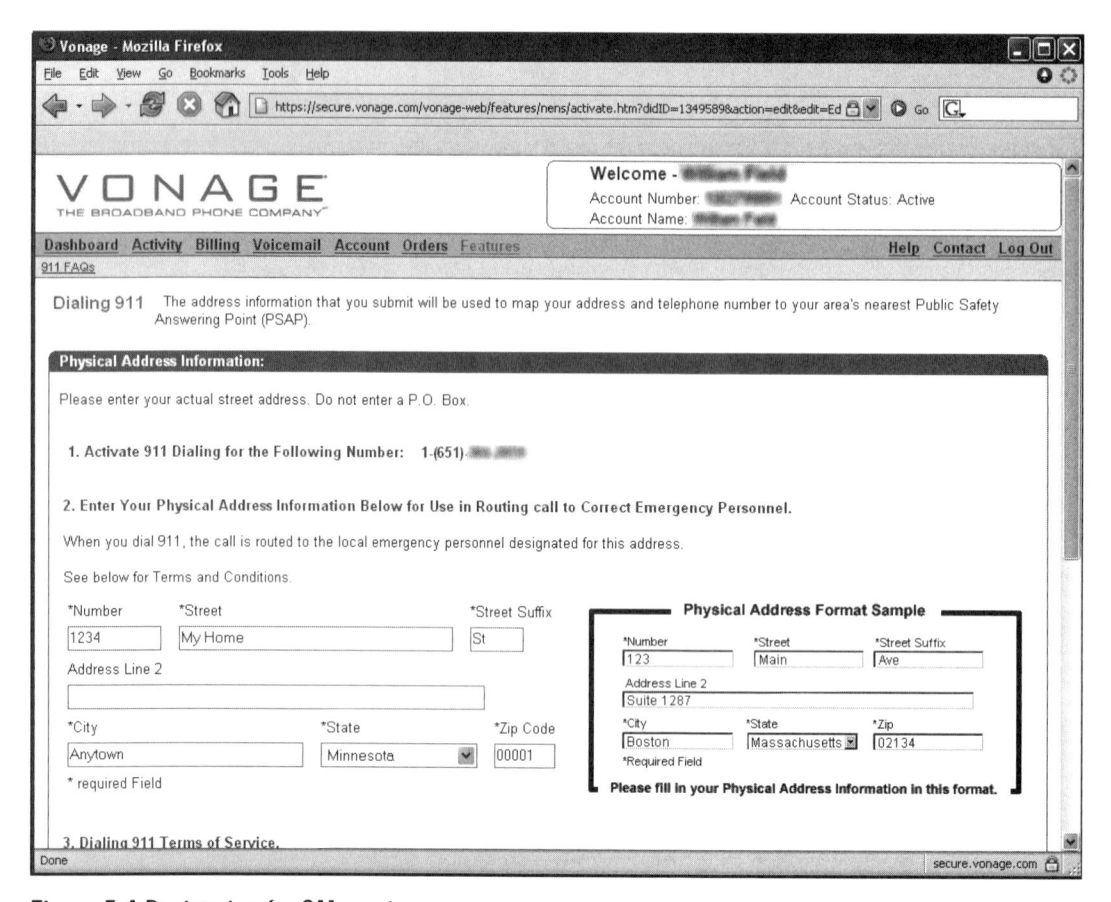

Figure 5.4 Registering for 911 service

To test your 911 service:

1. Dial 911, and when an operator answers, immediately inform him or her that this is not an emergency and that you are verifying the ability of your Internet phone to access emergency services.

2. Ask the operator whether he or she received your name and address information with your call. If so, you have access to enhanced 911 (E-911) services.

3. As soon as you have assessed the operator's ability to assist you in the event of an emergency, thank him or her, and hang up.

RESOLVING 911 PROBLEMS

If your 911 test uncovers a problem, you need to work with your VoIP provider to get it solved as quickly as possible. Consider a couple of likely scenarios:

No answer

You might call 911 only to have the phone ring without answer. If this is the case, call again during normal business hours in your community to see whether the phone is answered then. When someone does answer, inquire whether there is a better choice for emergency dialing. If so, provide this number to your VoIP provider's technical support staff, which will configure the number into your service.

WHAT IS E-911?

Enhanced 911 (E-911) is a level of 911 service provided by many incumbent local phone companies. The companies maintain this system with the support of 911 access fees on your home phone line. This service provides your name and address information to the PSAP during a 911 call, allowing emergency personnel to identify you even if you are unable to speak.

VoIP providers are currently gaining access to E-911 networks for their subscribers. In some localities (most notably, Rhode Island), they have offered this service to their subscribers for some time; in others, they have met with some resistance from the incumbent phone companies. In May 2005, the Federal Communications Commission ordered the incumbent carriers to open their infrastructure to VoIP providers. Starting in August 2005, VoIP providers will have access to this infrastructure in most areas.

The FCC continues to monitor this situation and is seeking ways to eliminate the need for registration for mobile VoIP users.

Incorrect PSAP

The party that answers your call might tell you that there is a better number to call in the event of an emergency. In this case, forward this number to your VoIP provider's technical support staff.

TRAVELING WITH 911

If you choose to bring your TA on a trip to make free calls from the road, be sure to consider the effect this will have on 911 dialing. If you will be staying in a place where you might have need of your own 911 services, be sure to register your current location on your provider's Web site.

ALTERNATIVES TO 911 DIALING

Some services may not provide 911 services yet; others might not be able to locate a satisfactory PSAP for your service. In these cases, you might have to access emergency services in other ways. Consider the following two options:

Use your cell phone

Your cell phone has access to 911 networks as part of your subscription. Many cell phones can actually transmit global positioning data to 911 operators to help them locate you in the event of an emergency.

Program local police and fire departments into your speed dial

You can also program the dispatch numbers of your local police and fire departments into your phone's speed dial. This will allow you to access these resources directly in the event of an emergency.

Local number portability (LNP)

One of the attractions of VoIP for most people is the ability to continue using your existing phone number after the switch. This process, called *local number portability (LNP)*, was initially ordered by the FCC to allow cellular phone carriers to acquire customers from other carriers without causing disruption to the subscriber's contact list. This portability was extended to numbers from traditional phone companies being transferred to cellular phones and now to VoIP phones.

ACTIVATING LNP

LNP can be initiated by your service provider at your request. Your provider will notify the local carrier that you want to port your number to its service. When the port takes place, the phone company will disconnect your local phone.

LNP is not available in all areas, and not all carriers offer LNP to their subscribers. In either case, you might be compelled to choose a new number.

WHEN LNP DOESN'T WORK

Occasionally, a provider offers LNP only to discover that it cannot perform the service for you. In this case, the provider usually cheerfully refunds your money and cancels your service. If this is not the case, be sure to remind the provider politely that LNP was part of why you chose its service and that you don't appreciate a bait-and-switch. This approach usually helps a provider decide to provide a refund.

AN ALTERNATIVE TO LNP

Some phone companies offer call-forwarding or referral services as part of their service cancellation. This usually costs you an activation fee, but it will provide your new number to callers whom you may not have notified about your number change.

Calling-feature setup

In addition to registering your 911 service and porting your phone number, there are calling features that you can activate and configure for your service (**Figure 5.5**). In this section, I look at a few of these services and describe their configuration.

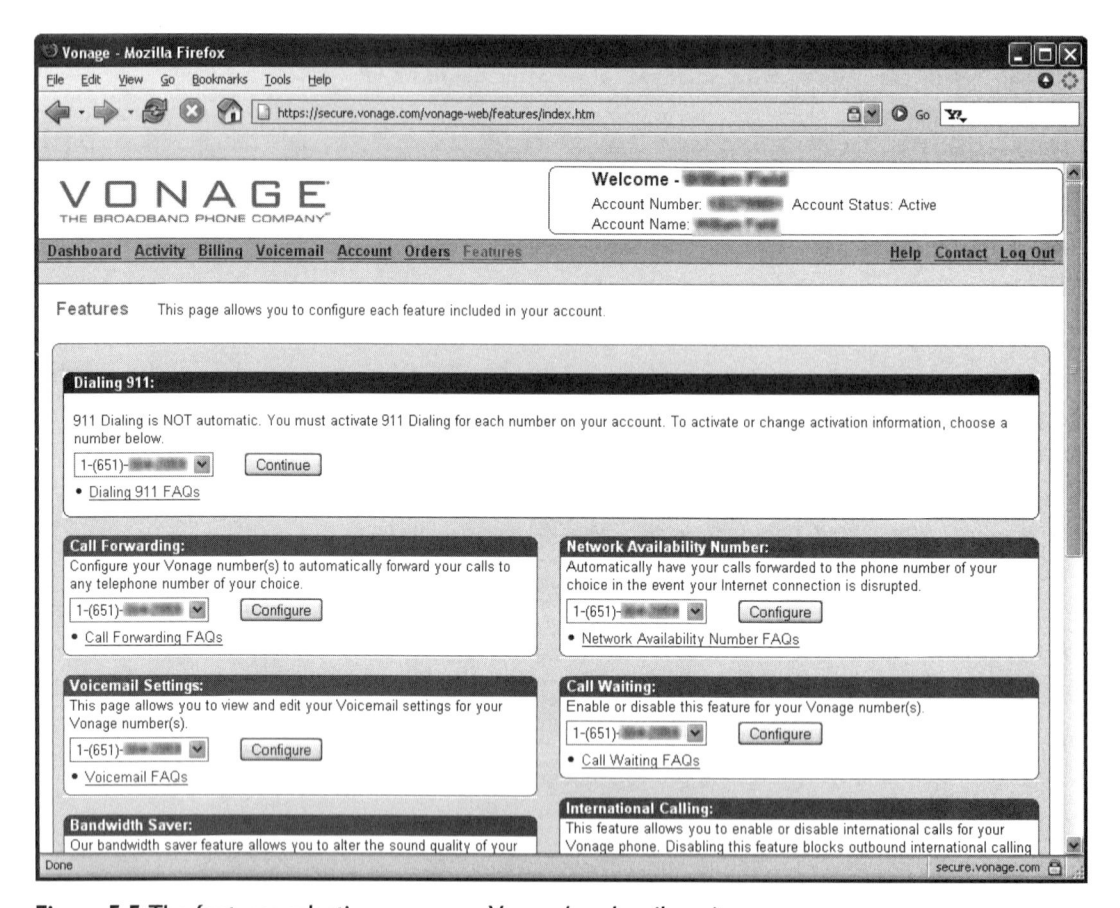

Figure 5.5 The features-selection screen on Vonage's subscriber site

VOICE MAIL

Many services allow you to configure your voice-mail feature either by phone or via the Web (**Figure 5.6**). Typically, this process involves activating the service, which uses a default greeting. If you choose to change your greeting, you use your telephone to record the new one.

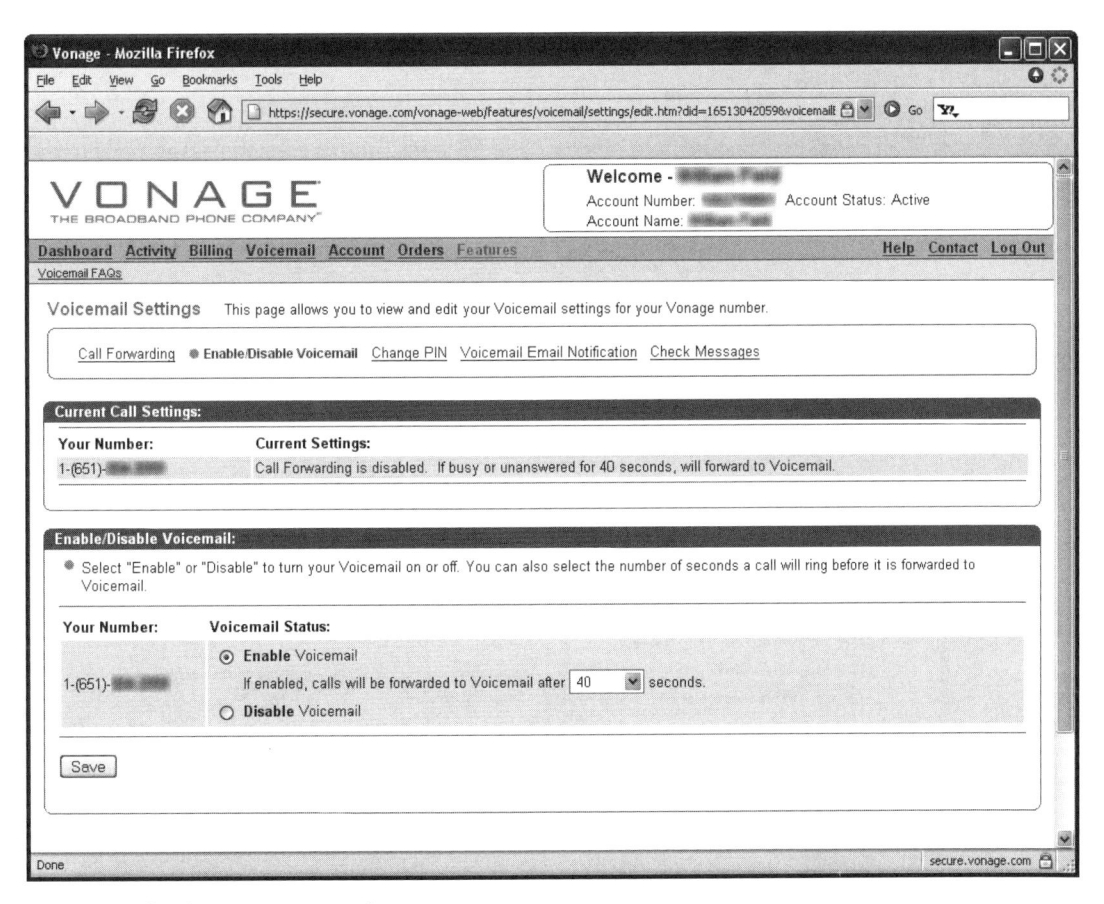

Figure 5.6 Configuring voice mail

You can collect messages by using your home telephone or by calling an access number when you're away from home. Most services also allow you to listen to voice-mail messages online (**Figure 5.7**). Your VoIP provider will alert you via e-mail when you have received a new voice-mail message.

CALL FORWARDING AND "FIND ME" SERVICES

Many related features fall under the heading of "call forwarding." Among these are the following.

Call forwarding

The standard call-forwarding feature will route incoming calls to any number you choose. If you do not answer, the call is handled by the destination number's voice-mail system or (if voice mail is unavailable at that number) routed to your own voice mail.

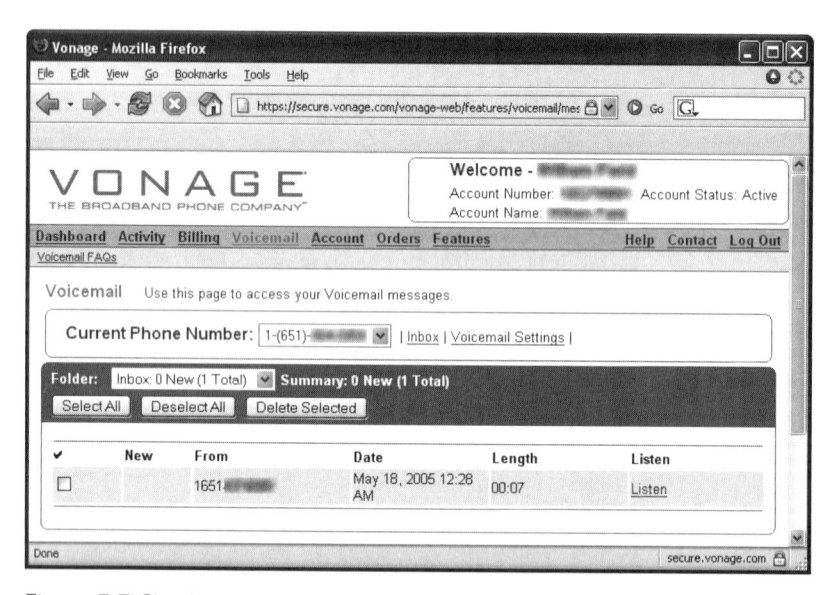

Figure 5.7 Checking voice mail online

Simultaneous ring

This feature (also discussed later in this chapter) simultaneously rings more than one phone number to locate you quickly. If you do not answer, the call is routed to voice mail.

Call hunting

This feature rings a series of numbers you select in sequence. The idea is that you will be at one of these numbers when the call comes in. If you are not, the call is routed to voice mail.

These services can be activated by phone or by Web. The Web configuration tools let you quickly set up what could take you several minutes entering codes and numbers by phone (**Figure 5.8**).

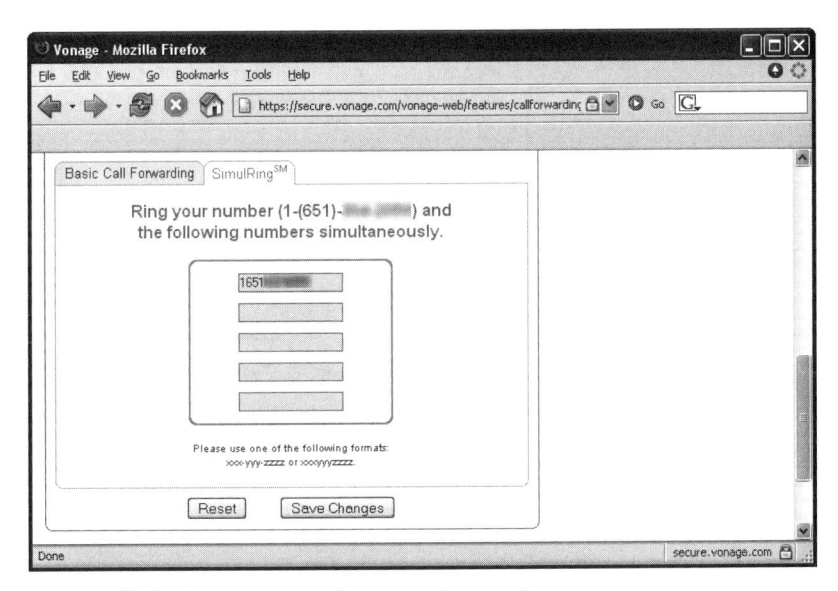

Figure 5.8 Configuring a simultaneous-ring service

FALLBACK NUMBER

In the event of a provider's network outage or your own loss of Internet service (such as during a power outage), you might elect to have your calls routed to an alternative phone number. You usually configure this feature configured on your provider's Web site (**Figure 5.9**).

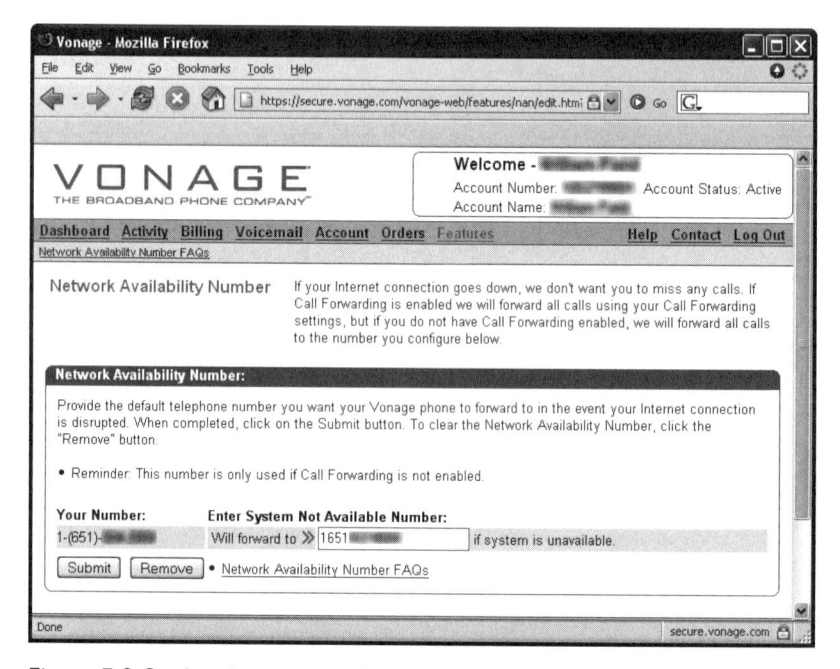

Figure 5.9 Configuring a network-outage fallback number

OTHER FEATURES

Each service provider has a list of its own features that require configuration (**Figure 5.10**). As you learn more about these features, you will be able to access configuration menus for them on your provider's Web site.

Postactivation Setup   CHAPTER FIVE   93

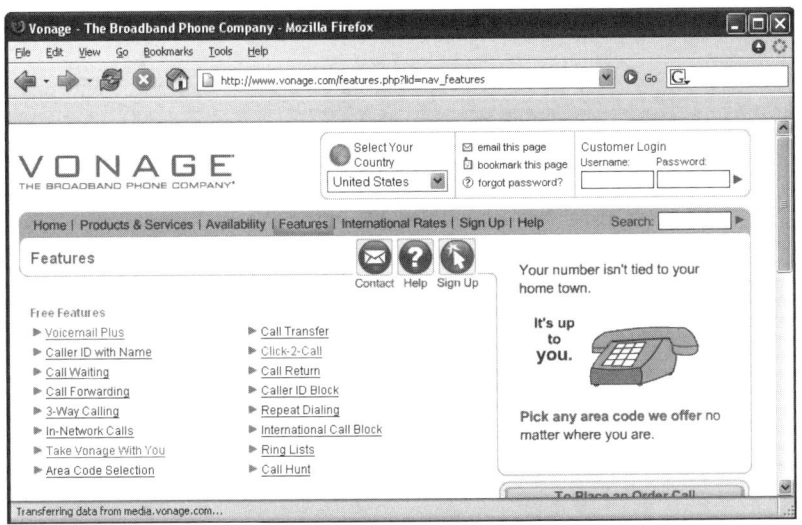

Figure 5.10 Additional features may require configuration to give you the most from your service.

> **TIP**
>
> Second lines can be distributed over your home phone cables. Check out "Distributing the Telephone Signal" in Chapter 4 for more information.

Additional lines

VoIP service providers offer additional-line options at a discount from their regular single-line charge. These lines can have local phone numbers or can be configured to use phone numbers from other areas, allowing you to offer virtually free calls to friends, family members, and business associates living in other communities.

To configure an additional line, simply sign up on your VoIP provider's Web site. The service will configure your TA to accept the second-line option. All that is required after that is to plug a phone into the Line 2 port on your TA.

Fax services

Merely an additional line to your VoIP provider, a fax line can be added for a monthly fee. The principal difference with a fax line is that it uses a high-quality codec to ensure correct signaling.

Blended services

The network and telephone convergence of VoIP services makes many interesting features available to VoIP users.

CLICK TO CALL

One blended service is the Click to Call feature offered by many providers. This service allows you to initiate calls from within your contact manager (usually, Microsoft Outlook).

Here's how Click to Call works:

1. The Click to Call software signals the VoIP provider's system to initiate the call.
2. Your phone begins to ring.
3. As soon as you pick up your phone, the system completes the call, and your called party's phone begins to ring.
4. Your called party answers, and you continue as with a normal call.

The advantage to services like Click to Call is the elimination of misdialing. You can initiate calls to a large contact list without looking each number up and dialing it manually.

SIMULTANEOUS RING

Another convergence enable feature is the simultaneous-ring feature offered by many providers. This feature will ring two or more phones simultaneously, connecting your call to the first phone that answers. Try that with a traditional phone!

Softphone service options

Many broadband phone services allow subscribers to access their systems both with TAs and softphones. This option enables subscribers to access Internet phone service at home and from computers in the office or on the road.

SETTING UP THE X-PRO SOFTPHONE FOR VONAGE

For an additional fee, Vonage offers subscribers the X-PRO SoftPhone software for use with its service. This software allows you to take the show on the road without bothering with disconnecting and reconnecting your TA at each stop. Simply install the softphone on a laptop computer, and use it at any Internet hotspot or hotel room with broadband Internet service.

The process of installing the X-PRO software is straightforward. After adding the feature to your subscription, you download the software and install it on your computer.

To install the X-PRO SoftPhone for Vonage:

1. Download and execute the X-PRO SoftPhone installation package.
2. Follow the steps in the installation wizard (**Figure 5.11**).

> **NOTE**
>
> The X-PRO SoftPhone is an additional line on your service. It has its own number and pool of minutes.

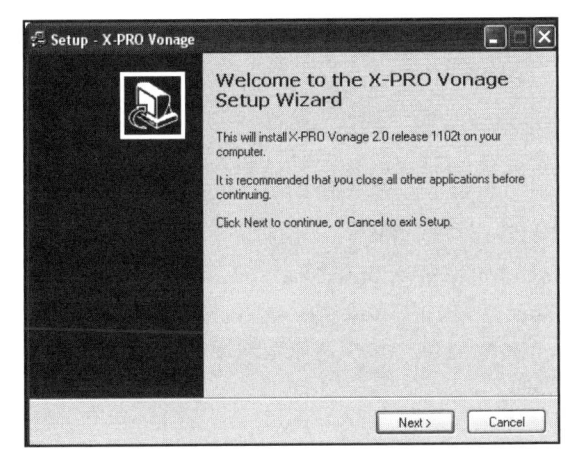

Figure 5.11 The X-PRO SoftPhone installation wizard

3. When the installation is complete, the softphone launches the Audio Tuning Wizard; follow the steps of this wizard to configure your computer's speakers and microphone.

> **NOTE**
>
> BroadVoice's Bring Your Own Device (BYOD) option allows you to activate its service for as little as $9.95 with your existing softphone software from XTen or EyeP.

4. When the Audio Tuning Wizard is complete, the softphone asks you to enter the phone number and password provided by Vonage after signup (**Figure 5.12**).

   After you enter this information, the softphone will be ready to use.

Figure 5.12 Logging into a softphone service

USING SOFTPHONES WITH BROADVOICE

Rather than requiring a separate number, BroadVoice allows you to use a softphone as your main phone. You can also choose to use Microsoft's Messenger communications software as an additional phone with your BroadVoice service for a small additional fee.

Installing Softphone-Only Services

Providers like Skype and Pulver's Free World Dialup are designed for softphones alone. Although the services may use optional USB handsets for control and communications, the telephone functionality is provided by the softphone software itself.

This section looks at the configuration of one of these services.

Installing and configuring the Skype softphone service

Skype has created its own proprietary softphone application, which combines many of the features of VoIP and instant messaging in one place. This application enables multimedia communications and gives users unprecedented capabilities.

To install Skype on your computer:

1. Download the Skype software from www.skype.com.

    You can choose among Windows, Macintosh, Linux, and PocketPC versions.

2. Execute the installation package to launch the Skype Setup Wizard (**Figure 5.13**), and follow the steps to complete the installation.

Figure 5.13 The Skype Setup Wizard

3. When the installation is complete, you will see a signup page
   (**Figure 5.14**); complete your information on this page.

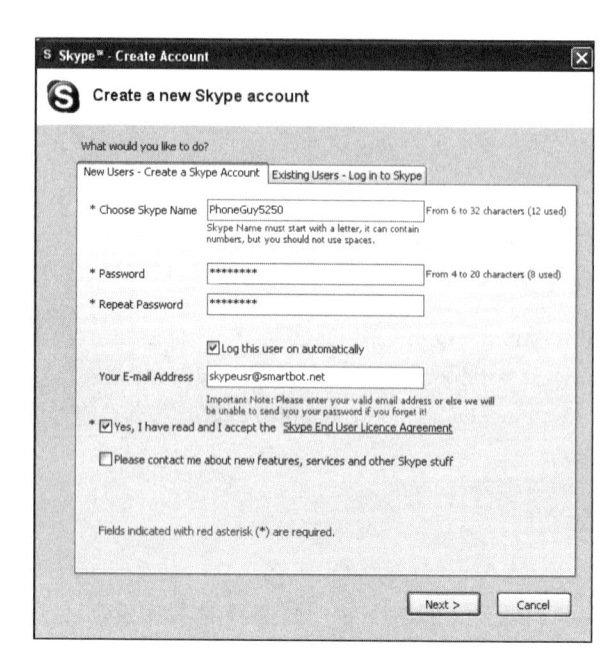

Figure 5.14 The Skype service requires a free subscription to access basic functionality.

4. Next, you are given the option of creating a user profile to tell other Skype users about yourself; complete or cancel this screen.

5. Use the Getting Started Wizard to import contacts, make a test call, and locate other Skype users (**Figure 5.15**).

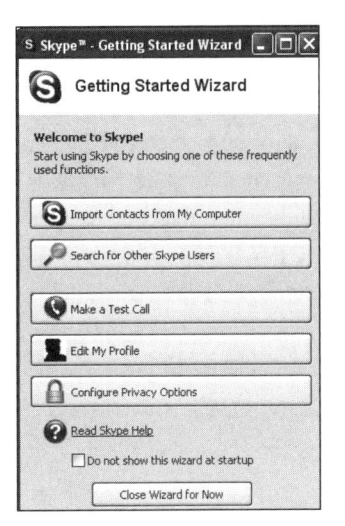

Installing Softphone-Only Services   CHAPTER FIVE   99

Figure 5.15 Using the Skype Getting Started Wizard, you can find old friends and import contacts.

6. After completing the Getting Started Wizard, you see the Skype main screen (**Figure 5.16**), where you can make calls or initiate chat sessions.

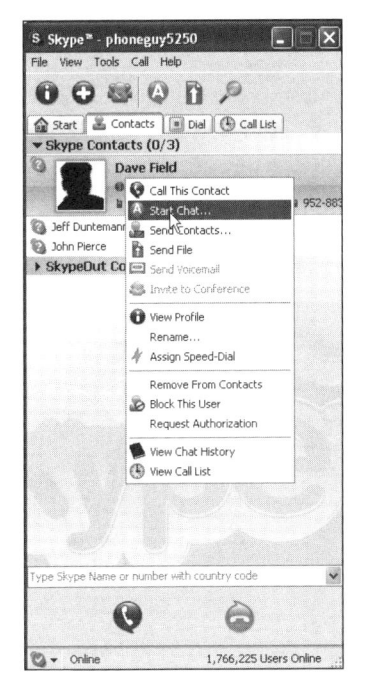

Figure 5.16 The Skype main screen

Integrate messaging and communications with Skype

With the unified communications of Skype, you can make voice calls, text-chat, and send files all at the same time. This multimedia communications ability is something you just cannot achieve with common telephones. In fact, the power of this medium will take some getting used to. Spend a little time chatting with Skype veterans to get a handle on how they communicate. It is an eye-opening experience.

Testing Your Internet Phone

If you're like me, you want to complete your installation by getting out on the road and seeing what this baby can do! There are testing sites that can help you determine how your service is performing. Testing allows you to spot potential problems before they affect your communications.

Bandwidth testing

For those who might have dropped into this chapter, welcome. I discussed bandwidth testing in earlier chapters, but it makes sense to test again after your service is installed. This testing will help you spot any service-quality issues that may have been introduced by the addition of your new hardware devices.

Sites such as Bandwidth Place (www.bandwidthplace.com) offer broadband bandwidth testing. A quick Google search for "bandwidth test" will give you a list of other testing sites. Refer to Table 3.1 in Chapter 3 for more information about how much bandwidth you should have.

Voice-quality testing

Now that your service is active, you can perform some voice-quality tests. You can make test calls to family members and friends, or you can use the services of an organization such as TestYourVoIP.com. These free testing services test the call quality of your system. Especially interesting is the Golden Phone service (**Figure 5.17**), which records an actual VoIP call and grades the quality of the reception.

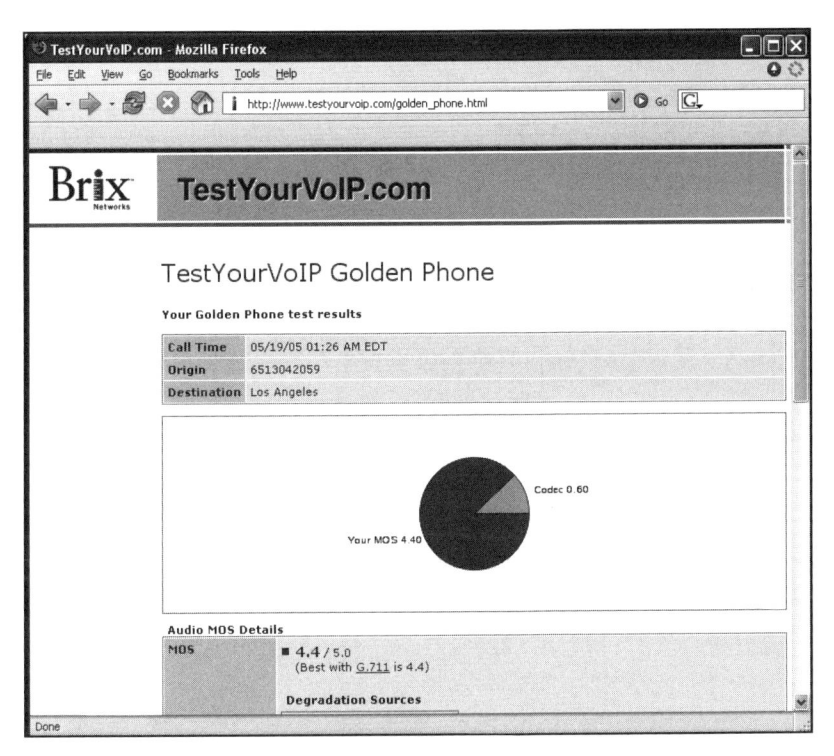

Figure 5.17 Golden Phone test results

Dealing with poor test results

If your voice-test results are not to your liking, you can make some changes to improve your scores.

ALTERNATIVE CODECS

If you are using a low-bandwidth (Bandwidth Saver) protocol such as G.729 or G.726, consider changing to G.711. This will often improve your service scores. Alternatively, try a different low-bandwidth codec. It may make a difference in your performance while keeping your bandwidth low.

QUALITY OF SERVICE (QOS) SETTINGS

If your TA is located behind a router, you might have to enable Quality of Service (QoS) settings on your router to let the TA appropriate more bandwidth during calls.

Another alternative would be to move the TA to the Internet side of your router. This may cause problems with your Internet connection, however, so check with your ISP before taking this step.

BANDWIDTH CONCERNS

If you simply have low bandwidth, you might have to upgrade your Internet service to gain additional bandwidth. Your Internet access provider will often have a higher-bandwidth service you can try. You might also consider changing Internet access providers.

Bringing It All Together

Well, you have come full circle. You've analyzed service options, selected and installed equipment, and established service. In the next few chapters, you will concentrate on getting the most from VoIP and customizing the service to suit your personality and style. I cover troubleshooting in more depth, discuss security, and even look at the future of VoIP communications.

For now, enjoy your new phone; I'll see you in Chapter 6.

CHAPTER SIX

Common VoIP Problems and Their Solutions

Not every Internet phone installation goes according to plan. If your installation runs into problems, you stand a better chance than most people to resolve it quickly, simply because you are more familiar with the inner workings of VoIP now. On the outside chance that the fix is not readily apparent, however, this chapter stands to assist you with the resolution of your issue.

I have organized problems by type, from problems caused by low or intermittent bandwidth to power and Internet outages. If you don't find the resolution here, I also show you where to go next for help.

IN THIS CHAPTER
Connection Issues **106**
Configuration Issues **112**
Hardware Problems **117**
Outages **121**
Additional Troubleshooting Resources **123**

Connection Issues

Because it relies so much on Internet bandwidth, VoIP will definitely let you know when all is not well with your Internet connection. You might have occasional gaps in your communications; dropped calls; or even fast busy signals, which are generated by your telephone adapter (TA) when it cannot locate your VoIP provider.

In this section, I cover the most common connection-related issues you might encounter.

Bandwidth

Bandwidth is the holy grail of Internet communications. Geeks like me often joke that they will work for bandwidth. It enables us to download programs, music, and movies without long waits. It allows us to communicate in real time using voice and video. When it is gone, we are left with jerky pictures, spotty audio, and slow Web pages.

Insufficient bandwidth affects your VoIP communications by starving your voice codecs and impeding signaling protocol function. In extreme cases, you may find it impossible to make or receive calls.

USING ALTERNATIVE CODECS

One strategy for dealing with bandwidth challenges is to use alternative codecs designed to use less bandwidth. You can cut your demands on your Internet connection from 90 Kbps to as little as 30 Kbps by choosing a low-bandwidth codec.

To change your codec, you might have to use your VoIP provider's Web site or configure settings in your TA. The exact procedure will vary by provider.

To change the codec for Vonage, you can access the Bandwidth Saver configuration page on the Vonage customer Web site (**Figure 6.1**).

> **NOTE**
>
> If you select low bandwidth settings, you may override them when dialing by dialing the *99 code before making a call. This allows you to have bandwidth-saving settings for most uses but program your fax machine to dial *99 to enable high quality for better fax transmissions.

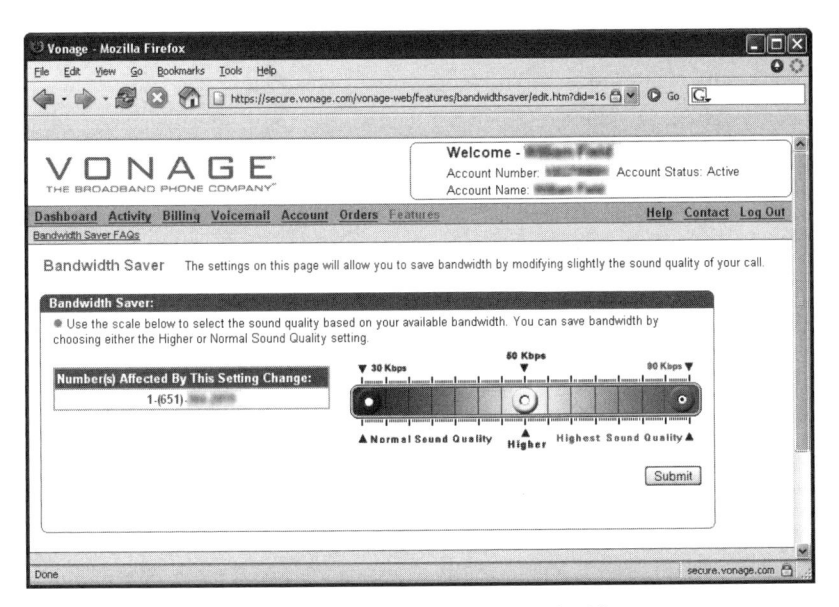

Figure 6.1 Changing Bandwidth Saver settings on the Vonage customer Web site

MANAGING QOS SETTINGS FOR GATEWAYS

TAs need a certain amount of bandwidth to be able to do their job. How you connect your TA to your network can affect your calls. If your TA is connected behind a gateway, for example, it will share Internet bandwidth with any other computers and devices that also use the gateway. Uploading or downloading large files during a call can cause problems unless you can configure your gateway to reserve bandwidth for your VoIP calls. This reservation process is called *quality of service (QoS) management*.

108 CHAPTER SIX Common VoIP Problems and Their Solutions

By designating one port that has preferential service levels, you can effectively reserve bandwidth for VoIP communications (**Figure 6.2**). This reservation is effective whenever there is traffic on that port. At other times, all other ports have unrestricted use of your gateway's bandwidth.

Gateway QoS configuration varies by manufacturer. Check your user manual to learn how to set QoS on your gateway.

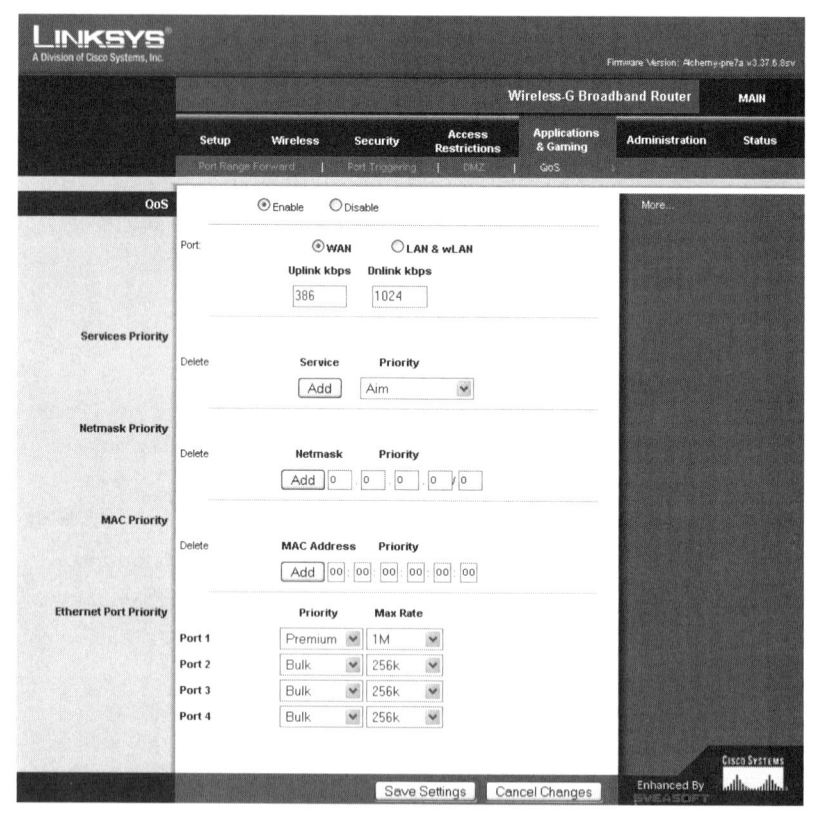

Figure 6.2 A Linksys WRT54G gateway configured to provide QoS preference to Port 1

MANAGING QOS FOR COMBINATION TA/GATEWAY DEVICES

Gateways that include TA functionality include QoS settings that can be set to provide QoS preference to the VoIP potion of the device over the network ports. The Linksys RT31P2 allows you to enable QoS separately for the voice portion of the device or the network portion of the device (**Figure 6.3**). Enabling QoS for voice will cause the TA portion of the device to receive preference for bandwidth allocation.

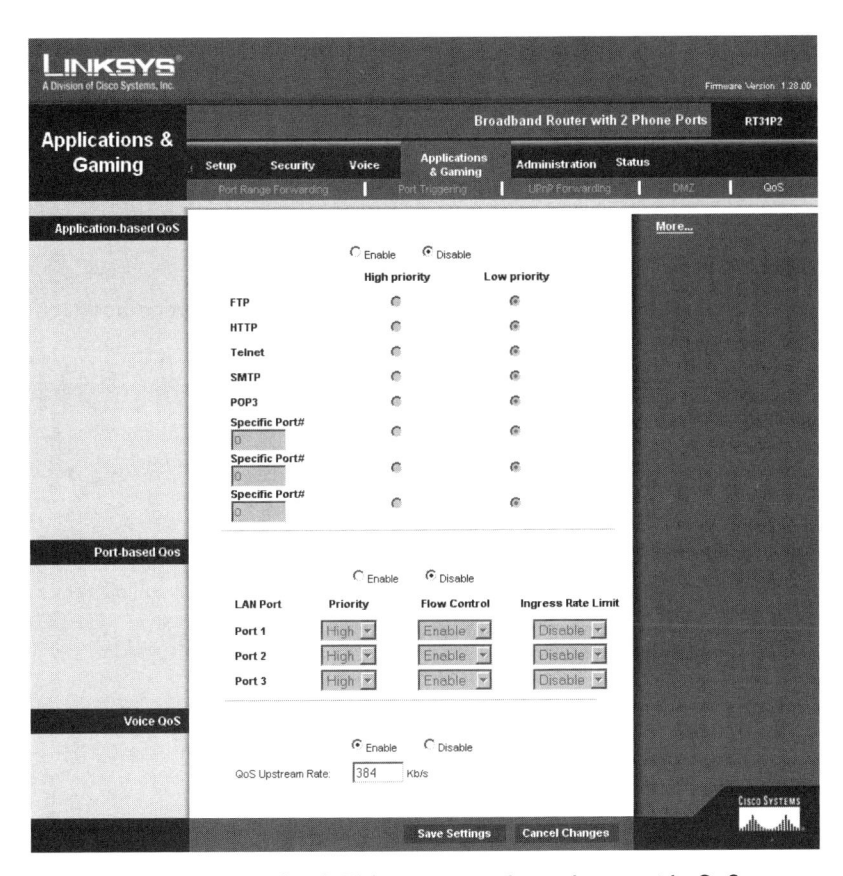

Figure 6.3 A Linksys RT31P2 TA/gateway configured to provide QoS preference for voice

Intermittent connection loss

Occasionally, you will have calls drop for no apparent reason. If this happens once a week or less, it may not be a reason for concern (probably just stray radiation from outer space!). If it happens more frequently, however, you might consider the possible causes listed in this section.

PACKET LOSS

Internet Protocol (IP) relies on the delivery of pieces of data called *packets* to make communications successful. When packets do not reach their intended destination, they leave a gap in the data reception. Drop a few packets, and you might miss a few milliseconds of conversation. Drop half of all packets, and you will probably lose the call.

There can be many reasons for packet loss. Almost all of them will be traceable to problems with your Internet access provider or loss of an Internet router between you and your VoIP provider. If you wait an hour and everything is fine, chances are that the downed router has recovered or has been taken from active routes on the Internet. Longer outages probably point to issues closer to home and should be the topic of a call to your Internet access provider's support line.

If packet loss is a frequent problem with your Internet service, you might consider finding a new one. Check out other providers in your area. Check their reviews on Broadbandreports.com, if possible. Ask for a trial period during which you can evaluate the provider's service before canceling your current one. If the dropped calls go away, make the switch.

PPPOE ISSUES

Point to Point Protocol over Ethernet (PPPoE) is the means that many Internet access providers use to prove you are an authentic customer when you connect to their systems. A user name and password are typically programmed into the Internet modem or your gateway device and sent to the provider's system when you connect.

Many Internet providers limit the length of time you can remain online when no traffic is being passed. Because PPPoE connects so quickly, providers can safely drop your connection, and you'll never notice. By the time you have launched your Web browser to surf the Web, the PPPoE connection is reestablished, and you can happily surf away.

This is not the case with VoIP, however. What if you were to receive an incoming call while your connection is down? You're right: Nothing. It is also possible that an improperly configured PPPoE setup might drop your connection even when you are using it. If you are browsing the Web, you might notice a few seconds of delay loading a page but might not think anything of it. If you are on a VoIP call, you will definitely notice. You may even have calls drop out as frequently as every minute or so.

Check your PPPoE settings, if you can (**Figure 6.4**). If you have the ability to enable Keep Alive settings, try doing that, and see whether the connection stays up. If it still drops periodically, call your Internet provider's support line to enlist help with determining the reason for the connection loss.

UNSTABLE CONNECTION

If your connection never drops completely, but you seem to have intermittent periods of poor communications, check the QoS settings of your gateway. Intermittent downloads for antivirus software updates, incoming e-mail, instant messaging updates, and other causes can sap the bandwidth from your VoIP sessions if QoS is not ready to protect it.

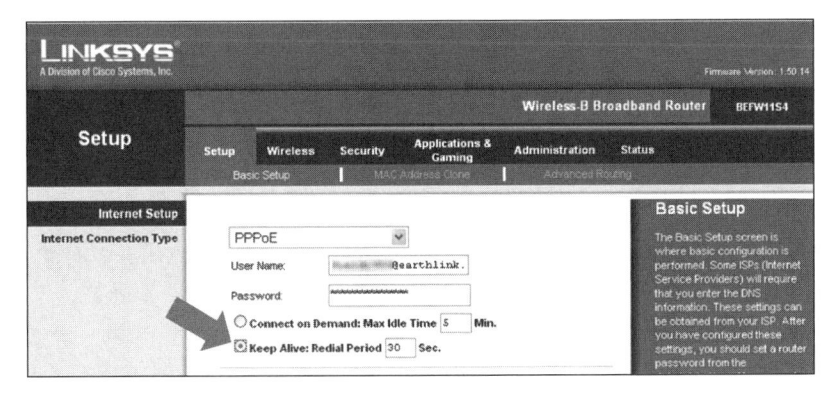

Figure 6.4 Enabling Keep Alive settings on a Linksys gateway

Configuration Issues

> **TIP**
>
> If you need to know more about home networking than I cover here, Peachpit Press offers books that cover this topic in much more detail.

Many potential issues can arise from improper configuration of your Internet devices or TA. Most of these improper settings result in outright failure, but some may be more subtle. Most of the subtle items, such as QoS and PPPoE Keep Alive, were discussed in the previous section. Let's take a look now at the show-stoppers.

Gateway configuration

Perhaps you bought an Internet gateway at the same time you purchased your VoIP kit. Maybe your gateway was included in the VoIP kit (TA/gateway combo). Either way, you should be aware of several settings that might make your gateway installation more challenging. Your Internet access provider can assist you if you have any questions about the actual values to use for certain settings.

INTERNET ADDRESS CONFIGURATION

Most Internet access providers automatically assign the Internet (or external) address for your gateway. If this is not the case, and you must set an address manually, you will be given a configuration guide that specifies the address to use for the gateway.

Internal addresses—those addresses assigned to devices inside the gateway—are left to your discretion. Most gateways use a feature called *Dynamic Host Configuration Protocol (DHCP)* to assign IP addresses automatically to computers and devices such as TAs on your internal network (**Figure 6.5**). All you have to do is ensure that each device is set to accept these addresses. Consult the user manual for your TA to determine its default setting and for directions on changing the setting if necessary.

Likewise, your PC usually obtains its own address automatically from DHCP, but use your system's help screens for assistance on setting the address manually, if desired.

Configuration Issues   **CHAPTER SIX**   113

Figure 6.5 Configuring a Linksys gateway to provide IP addresses to network devices

PPPOE SETTINGS

In addition to Keep Alive settings, discussed in "PPPoE issues" earlier in this chapter, PPPoE requires you to provide a user name and password before communications can be established (**Figure 6.6**). Enter the user name and password specified by your Internet provider in this configuration screen. After saving your settings, wait a few minutes before testing your connection, as it may take some time for your gateway to locate and connect with the appropriate systems.

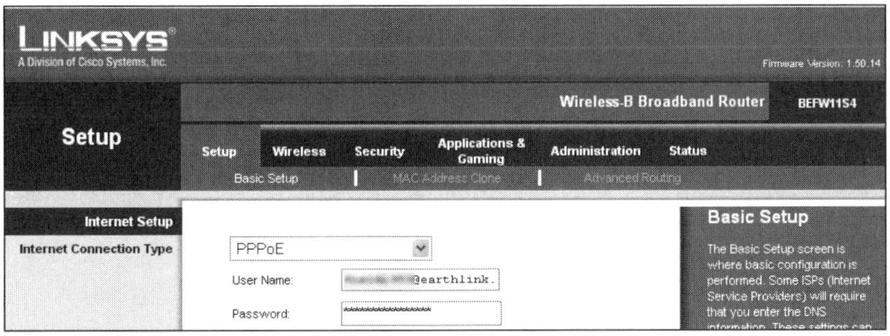

Figure 6.6 Setting the PPPoE user name and password

MAC SPOOFING

Some Internet access providers register the media access control (MAC) ID of your computer when you subscribe to their services. If your access provider is expecting the registered MAC and does not see it, you will not be able to connect. Gateway vendors have cleverly bypassed this issue by designing their products to pretend that they *are* your PC (**Figure 6.7**). This process, called *MAC cloning* or *MAC spoofing*, uses the computer's registered MAC ID that you configure into the gateway when communicating with the Internet provider's systems. By using your PCs MAC ID, the gateway effectively fools the provider's network into thinking that your computer is making the connection. The reality is, you now have an entire network sharing the same address!

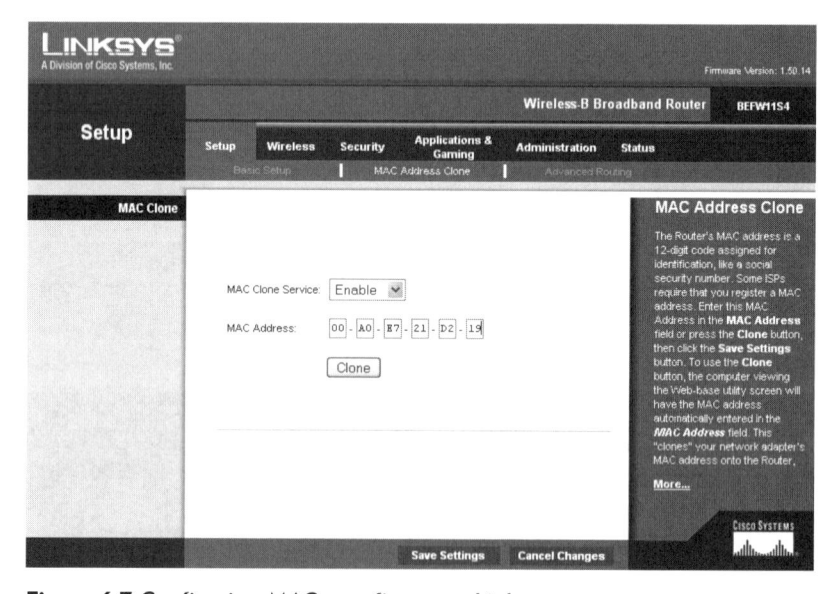

Figure 6.7 Configuring MAC spoofing on a Linksys gateway

WHAT IS A PORT?

To communicate over the internet, computers and other devices must have addresses. The IP address you configure into your PC allows remote computers to communicate with it.

But what happens when you want to use the Web and e-mail at the same time? How would your system know which incoming packets are for the Web browser and which are e-mail?

The brilliant minds that thought up the Internet had an answer for that, too. They defined numbered *ports*, which are used in addition to your IP address to create *sockets*—discrete channels for communication. When you communicate with a Web server, you use port 80. Most e-mail uses ports 25 and 110. By using sockets, your system can manage dozens, if not hundreds, of communication channels at the same time.

Following are some other well-known ports:

20-21	File Transfer Protocol (FTP)
23	Telnet
53	Domain Naming System (DNS)
67	Dynamic Host Configuration Protocol (DHCP)
194	Internet Relay Chat (IRC)
443	Secure Sockets Layer (SSL, for secure Web browsing)

PORT-RANGE FORWARDING

When you place your TA behind a gateway, sometimes the firewall functionality of the gateway restricts your ability to connect to your VoIP provider. This is relatively rare, as most gateways are configured to allow all outbound communications, and your TA will communicate outbound first to initiate the connection with your VoIP provider.

If you do need to open your gateway to the TA, you will need to know which Internet ports are required for your service.

Most services use certain well-known port numbers for their communications. Those for your VoIP systems can be obtained from your VoIP provider's Web site or support staff. You probably will find port listings in the user guide for your TA as well. **Table 6.1** lists an example of ports used by a Linksys TA.

Table 6.1 Linksys PAP 2 Ports

Service	Ports	Protocol
DNS (Domain Naming System; address resolution)	53	UDP
TFTP (Trivial File Transfer Potocol; firmware updates)	69	UDP
SIP (Session Initiation Protocol; call setup and signaling)	5060-5061	UDP
RTP (Realtime Transport Protocol; communication after call setup)	10000-20000	UDP

TA configuration

The TA provided by your VoIP provider or included in your VoIP kit usually works right out of the box with no modification. Some exceptions are when your home network uses static (not dynamically assigned) IP addresses or more than one gateway device (not likely).

TAs usually have two methods of configuration: They can be configured via a Web browser by accessing a small Web server built into the device, or they can be programmed over your touchtone phone. Often, your VoIP provider will lock out the Web interface to be able to support your TA remotely from its central support department. If this is the case, you will be restricted to using the voice-response menu.

USING THE VOICE-RESPONSE MENU

When you use your TA's voice-response menu, follow the instructions carefully; they should be included in the user guide that comes with the device. You usually enter a code such as **** to access the voice-response menu. Then you use your keypad to access and change different settings.

SETTING IP ADDRESS AND GATEWAY SETTINGS MANUALLY

Using the voice-response menu, you can configure your TA to use a fixed IP address and fixed gateway address. Check the instructions that came with your TA for exact details on how to do this. Use an IP address that will be valid for your network and your gateway's address for the gateway address on your TA.

> **NOTE**
>
> Due to the nature of gateways, you will always have access to the networking portions of your gateway setup. Voice portions will be locked by your VoIP provider.

Hardware Problems

Sometimes, hardware devices simply fail. When this happens, it can appear to be related to configuration. The main difference between configuration and hardware failures is that for configuration issues, the system may never have worked properly or may have malfunctioned after a configuration change. With hardware failures, the system once worked and now doesn't, even though you changed nothing.

TA failure

TAs can fail occasionally. Sometimes, the failure is due to a faulty power supply or loss of wall power; at other times, the cause of the failure is less obvious. Perhaps an internal circuit failed, and the only indication you have is the failure of the device to connect to your VoIP provider.

The status lights on your TA may offer some indication of what the problem is. You can report the status of these lights to your VoIP provider's support staff to help them determine why your TA failed.

TIP

The process of issuing a replacement part is called *RMA* (for *returned merchandise authorization*). When you are asked to send in your old unit, be sure to ask for an RMA number. This code will ensure that your returned device is credited to your account and that you will not be charged for the replacement device.

NO POWER

When power is lost to the TA, you will see no lights at all. The cause may lie with the device's power supply module, or in the power strip or surge suppressor to which you have the device connected. Occasionally, you may lose wall power; in this case, you will probably notice several devices out at the same time. Most power issues can be isolated and repaired fairly quickly. If the power supply module is lost, however, you might have to call for a new one that will take some time to be delivered.

When you have no power lights, work your way from the TA device to the wall. Plug a small table lamp into the outlet the device uses on your power strip. If the lamp fails to light, plug it into the wall outlet. If the lamp does light, you will need to reset or replace your power strip.

If you determine that your power supply module is bad, call the manufacturer of your TA device to request a replacement. You might also be able to order a new module from your VoIP provider.

THE BLINKING LIGHTS ARE TRYING TO TELL YOU SOMETHING

If your TA's status lights are steady or blinking, you can safely rule out power failure. Call your VoIP provider to report the sequence of the blinking lights. Different blink rates or the blinking of certain lights while others are steady can be an indication of the cause of the malfunction. It could turn out to be a configuration issue or a hardware failure. If the status code reports a device failure, your provider will request that you send your TA in for replacement.

If your provider wants to replace your TA, inquire about an advance replacement. Getting the replacement unit in the mail before yours arrives in the shop will have you online much more quickly.

Home wiring problems

If you have chosen to distribute your Internet phone over your home's existing phone cables, you might run into one of the issues in this section. The remedies for these issues vary from simply reducing the number of connected phones to rewiring some of your wall jacks.

NOT ALL PHONES RING

To cause phones in your home to ring, your TA applies a ring voltage to the wires connecting it to your phones. If this voltage is raised above a certain level, it causes the phones in your home to begin ringing. Each phone draws a certain amount of electrical current off the line as it rings. If too many phones are connected, not all of them will receive enough electrical current to ring. The way to prevent this situation is to evaluate the ringer load of the phones on your system. By adding up these numbers and comparing the result with the TA's maximum ringer load, you will know if you are overloading the lines.

Most TAs are able to ring the equivalent of four or five old-style Bell telephones. The ringers of these phones were used as a baseline for the *Ringer Equivalence Number (REN)*—a relative rating of the current draw of an individual phone—and were given a REN of 1. If you inspect the manufacturers' tags on your phones, look for the term *REN* or *Ringer Equivalence*. These items will be listed as decimal numbers indicating the relative current draw required to activate a ring tone on that phone. Modern phones use as little as a few hundredths of the current required by an old-style phone. It is possible, therefore, to connect many of these devices to a TA.

If you suspect ringer-load issues, add up the REN values from all phones on the line. If the sum is more than 4, you might need to disconnect some phones or buy a ring booster device (**Figure 6.8**). A *ring booster* uses supplemental power to boost the ringer-load capacity of your system, allowing it to ring more telephones. Devices with ringer-load ratings of 15 or more are available online. Just Google "ring booster" for a list of Web sites selling these devices.

Figure 6.8 The Viking RG-10A Ring Booster is available from many online retailers.

NO DIAL TONE

If you receive a dial tone when you're connected directly into your TA but not from one or more phones on your home phone system, you will have to isolate improper wiring at some location in the system. It is best to approach this problem methodically, working your way out from the TA or known-good phone jacks.

If no jacks are working, check the wires in the jack to which you have connected the TA. If these wires are not properly connected, you have solved the problem. Check to be sure that the colors used in this jack are the same ones used in other jacks in your home. Refer to Chapter 4 for specific connection tips.

If some jacks work, check your connections in the distribution panel or demarcation point. One or more jacks may need to be connected into your system. Connect all like colors to interconnect all cables.

If you still do not get a dial tone everywhere, you will need to obtain a line tester for a few dollars at your local hardware store or home center (**Figure 6.9**). Use this device to test for disconnected wires and reversed wires at your phone jacks.

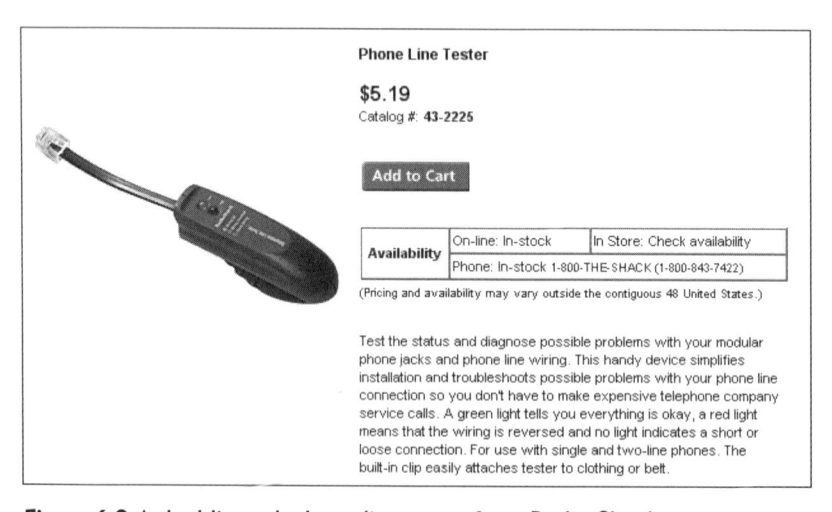

Figure 6.9 A dual-line telephone line tester from Radio Shack

SECOND LINE DOES NOT WORK

If you have activated the second line of your TA, you can distribute it throughout your home as well. If you followed the instructions in Chapter 4 for distributing your second line, and some or all jacks do not have a dial tone for the second line, check the wiring in each jack. If the jack where you connected the TA uses black and yellow or orange and white–orange wires for the second line, make sure that all other jacks in your home are wired the same way. In addition, make sure the cables that are connected in your junction box or demarcation point are interconnected to carry the signal in these wires to all jacks in the home.

To use a second line, you need either a two-line phone or a splitter jack that makes Line 2 available for a single-line phone (**Figure 6.10**).

Figure 6.10 Use a jack splitter similar to the Allen Tel AT173 two-line modular adapter to access both lines with a single-line phone.

If necessary, use a telephone line tester to test the connections in your two-line jacks for proper connections.

Outages

Sometimes, there is absolutely nothing you can do to maintain service. Power outages can kill the power the TA needs to operate, Internet outages can break the connection with the VoIP provider, and the service from your VoIP provider could be affected by conditions beyond its control.

There are actions you can take to minimize the effects of an outage, however, and I cover them in this section.

Power outage

Summer thunderstorms, rolling blackouts, and winter ice storms can cause power outages. With wireline services, you have come to expect that the telephone will still be operational (unless you are using a telephone that itself requires power from the wall). Because your TA requires wall power to operate, a power outage can knock out your phones as well.

There are steps you can take to ensure that you can still make and receive calls during a power outage. Let's look at them now.

UNINTERRUPTIBLE POWER SUPPLIES

Uninterruptible power supplies (UPS) use a battery to generate electricity to operate a computer or communications equipment during a power failure. A proper-size UPS can provide power for hours to operate your TA and Internet modem to sustain Internet phone service (**Figure 6.11**).

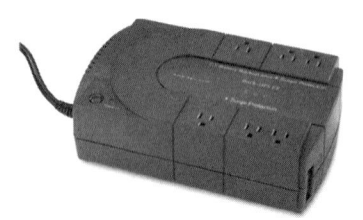

Figure 6.11 For $60, a UPS like the APC Back-UPS ES 500 can run small loads like modems and TAs for over an hour.

To select a UPS, you should consider the load that will be operating on it during a power failure. Total the current demand of the devices that will be connected, and choose a UPS that will sustain that demand for an hour or more. Many UPS manufacturers offer sizing tools on their Web sites and in big-box retail electronics stores.

Keep in mind that most UPS devices are designed to operate large loads, such as a computer and monitor, during an outage. If you are using the UPS solely for communications devices, you will not need a very large UPS to provide power for a reasonable length of time.

CALL FORWARDING

If the power outage drags on, and it looks like the UPS just won't make it, you can use call forwarding to send incoming calls to your cell phone or another line. Most VoIP providers offer this feature, as well as "find me" services that you can use to forward calls automatically to multiple phones, including cell phones, until the call is answered.

Internet and VoIP service outage

In the event of an Internet or VoIP provider outage, there is little you can do to reestablish service until the service returns. In this situation, you'll need to rely on preset "find me" services and voice mail. Having these services set up ahead of time will ensure that you can receive calls when an outage occurs.

Additional Troubleshooting Resources

Your VoIP provider will have telephone and online resources available to assist with installation and configuration issues. In addition, several Web sites are available to help with troubleshooting VoIP issues.

Among these are

- Fire the Phone Company Blog (www.firethephonecompany.info)
- The VoIP Wiki (www.voip-info.org/tiki-index.php)
- Vonage VoIP Forum (www.vonage-forum.com)
- Broadband Reports' VoIP Forum (www.dslreports.com/forum/voip)

Using what you have learned here and the resources of the people in these forums, there should be no problem you cannot solve.

CHAPTER SEVEN

VoIP Security

As is the tendency with new technologies, especially Internet technologies, security for Internet phone communications came as a bit of an afterthought. For once, however, it was not much of an afterthought. During the creation of the SIP protocol, security was becoming a buzzword in Internet circles. As a result, fairly decent safeguards were built into the design.

This is not to say that hackers will not find ways to mess with you. The game of cat and mouse goes on as we speak. Security researchers *(hackers)* discover vulnerabilities in Internet protocols, and those with malicious intent *(crackers)* make use of these discoveries to steal resources, harass users, and insomniate security administrators.

In this chapter, I answer your questions about VoIP security and show you things you can do to make your systems less inviting to the "black hats" out there.

IN THIS CHAPTER
Security Q&A **126**
Secure Your Internet Phone **131**
Learn More about VoIP Security **135**

> **NOTE**
>
> Although setting up a gateway for Internet security is beyond the scope of this book, good books are available to help with this task. For more information on the configuration of your gateway for VoIP, check out Chapters 4 and 6.

Security Q&A

Many questions arise when you consider the security of Internet phone communications. Many of these issues have affected landline and cell phones for years, but they crop up in new and interesting ways when the Internet is involved.

Let's discuss a few of these questions now.

Will VoIP open my network to intruders?

Short answer? Probably not.

Internet gateways are designed to open outbound connections to your VoIP provider on the demand of your TA. Attempts to communicate inbound without first being invited by the TA are not allowed. A properly configured gateway should appear as a black hole in the Internet, not responding to any attempts to access ports on the address held by the gateway (**Figure 7.1**).

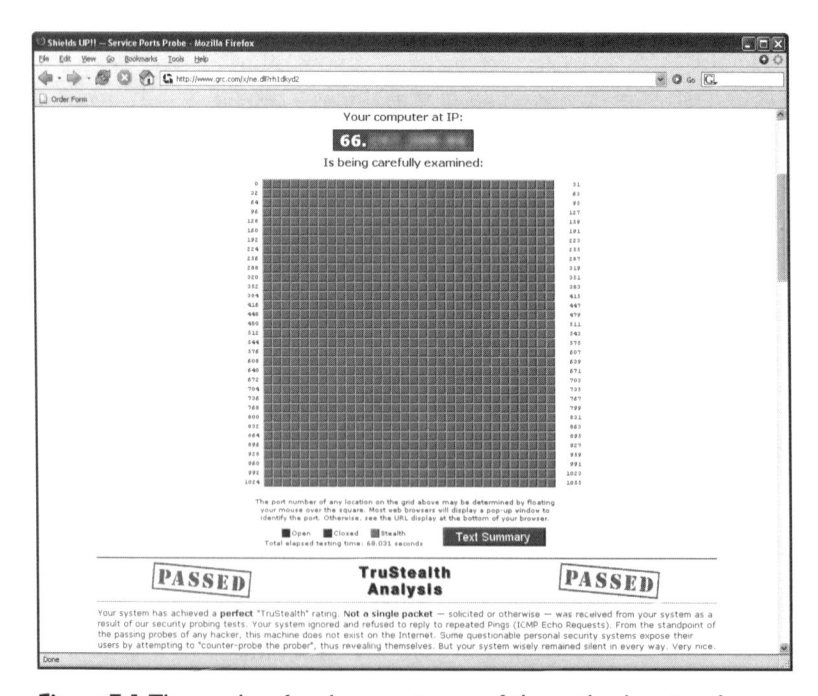

Figure 7.1 The results of a clean port scan of the author's network (image from grc.com)

Can others eavesdrop on my phone calls?

Once again, probably not. Not in real time, anyway.

Most Internet services connect you and a relatively small number of local users to a router owned by your Internet access provider. When your communications reach your Internet provider, they travel across large backbone networks to your VoIP provider. The chance that anyone on those large networks would (or could) monitor your data is small.

Of the users on your local node, anyone who would want to listen in must be able to capture and decode your VoIP packet stream—not impossible, but beyond the ability of most of the general population. At this point, it comes down to who your neighbors are. Anyone who is *that* interested could just as easily place a tap on your demarcation point some dark night (**Figure 7.2**). It's a heck of a lot easier to tap the local line of your telephone company than it is to configure a sniffer to catch your VoIP calls.

Figure 7.2 This $5 phone tapping device is available online.

What other types of attacks are VoIP phones subject to?

Those with too much time on their hands (crackers) have a number of attacks at their disposal that they can use to disrupt your Internet phone conversations. Notice that I say "disrupt." Though it may be difficult to listen in on a VoIP conversation, it is simple to break one up.

128 CHAPTER SEVEN VoIP Security

Crackers can command vast armies of Internet *bots*—computers that have been infiltrated with spyware and with programs that give crackers remote control, allowing them to direct traffic at specified Internet addresses. If your address is known to a cracker, he can use his bot fleet to swamp you with meaningless communications, effectively cutting off your ability to communicate with the rest of the Internet (**Figure 7.3**). This will definitely prevent you from using VoIP until the attack subsides.

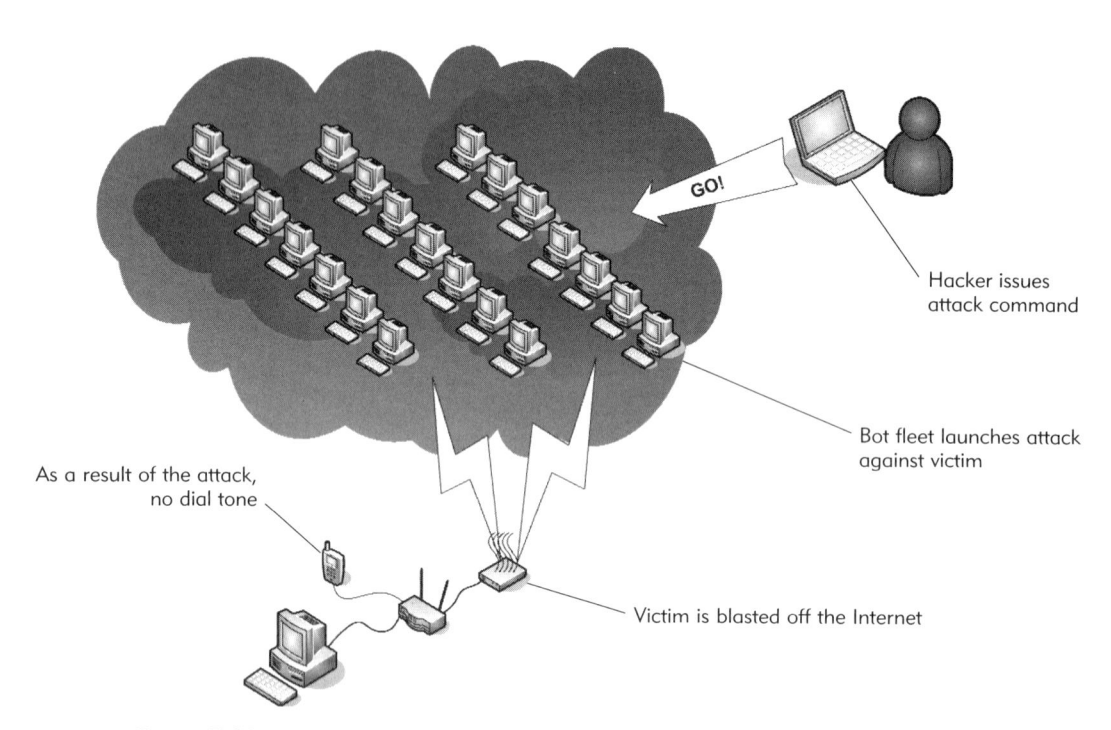

Figure 7.3 Victims of bot fleets can only wait for an attack to subside.

You might not even know you are under attack by a fleet of bots. You might think your Internet connection is simply down. If you do recognize the symptoms of an attack, you still might have difficulty persuading the support staff at your Internet provider to help. Although your provider can help you track down the source and block the attacks, that takes time and resources. By the time your provider has located the source, the cracker has usually lost interest and moved on to another victim. For this reason, it is sometimes best just to weather the storm.

Can anyone steal my minutes?

It is technically possible to craft communications that appear to come from your TA, enabling another party to access and use your VoIP minutes. This type of attack requires the attacker to know several things about you, such as your location, phone number, and IP address. Although these items can be sniffed from your communications, they require local access, and you will easily detect them when you see calls you did not make on your next bill.

With this and any other type of attack, you have to consider the probability that an attacker will target you. For most of us, these types of attacks are not very likely. For those who cannot take that chance (such as CEOs and nuclear scientists), a solution like encrypted VoIP, provided by your company or Uncle Sam, would be in order.

I use a wireless network. Is my VoIP secure?

Much has been said about wireless network security. Recently, large strides have been made to secure wireless networks from the black hats. Today, you can buy a consumer-grade wireless network gateway that employs 802.11i (also known as WPA2) security. This level of security uses rotating encryption keys to scramble your communications. Taken individually, a single data packet captured off the air can eventually be cracked. Even if the key eventually becomes known to the hacker, by that time, it will have long since been changed.

> **NOTE**
>
> Setup and configuration of 802.11i, WPA2, and WPA-PSK are too involved to deal with in these pages. For more information about these protocols, look for a book about wireless security. Make sure the book is a very recent one, as this field is always changing.

It is important to understand that these new encryption features apply only to devices released since the last quarter of 2004. Carefully read the specifications of your device to determine whether it supports 802.11i/WPA2. Older methods of encryption, such as WEP, have been cracked and are essentially no protection against a hacker who wants to see inside your network.

WHAT IS WPA2?

Now ratified as 802.11i, WPA2 is the standard being used for new consumer wireless equipment that has improved security capabilities. WPA2 devices use Advanced Encryption Standard (AES) encryption—the same currently being used by the U.S. government—to protect transmissions.

Businesses using 802.11i can set up complex authentication methods to ensure that users are authorized before being allowed to connect to the wireless network.

For home users, a variant of WPA2 called WPA-PSK allows you to set up WPA2 to operate in your home. This simplifies the process of configuration for this standard and offers very good protection against access by bad guys.

Some companies, such as Linksys, offer managed WPA2 security services with their new devices, allowing you to configure your wireless devices to check with a remote server on the Internet before allowing any user or device to access your wireless network. This gives a home user corporate-level security for a fraction of the price.

Secure Your Internet Phone

Now that I have scared you into rethinking Internet phones, let's look at some ways to protect yourself against some of the attacks that threaten your phones. In this section, I show you steps you can take to secure your Internet connection and your phone service.

Analyze the risks

Who are you talking to, and what are you saying? If the worst thing that passes your lips is some juicy gossip about a neighbor, chances are that VoIP security is fine for your needs. If, however, you deal with corporate trade secrets or nuclear launch codes, you will probably want something with a little more heft.

Like a shoe phone.

Let's put this in perspective. Standard phones can be tapped. Older cellular phones could be eavesdropped on (much to the chagrin of certain royal highnesses). The advent of personal communications service (PCS) technology made cellular communications much more secure but still not impenetrable. If you are comfortable with standard phones and cellular phones, feel safe with VoIP.

Use a gateway

One way to increase security—not only for VoIP calling, but also for all Internet communications—is to use a gateway that includes firewall functionality (**Figure 7.4**). Available from your local big-box electronics retailer or online from many merchants, these devices (manufactured by Linksys, Netgear, D-Link, and others) do a very good job of providing basic network protection.

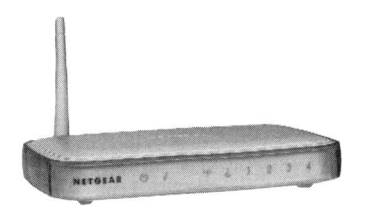

Figure 7.4 The Netgear WGR614 wireless broadband gateway includes a firewall and parental-control features.

NETWORK ADDRESS TRANSLATION (NAT)

The Internet gateway uses *network address translation (NAT)* to enable multiple connected internal devices to share your Internet connection. By using only one public Internet address, your *attack surface*—the portion of your network exposed to attack—is dramatically reduced.

NAT tracks all outbound and inbound communications, and ensures that the correct traffic is routed to each device on your network. As long as these devices are compatible with NAT, you should have no problems setting up this feature of your gateway.

FIREWALLS

Most gateways include firewall functionality to protect your network further. With a firewall, inbound communications must be in response to established outbound requests, or they will not be allowed to enter your network. Attempts to break in are silently discarded.

If you host services behind the firewall that rely on inbound traffic to initiate the connection (such as a Web site or a game server), you can manually designate open ports and the internal system that is to receive connection attempts on these ports. This method, called *port forwarding*, ensures that no unauthorized traffic enters your network. The internal system that receives the traffic needs to be monitored for unauthorized access attempts, however, and you should check frequently to be sure that the shared application on this system does not have any known vulnerabilities that have not been fixed. You can do this by checking frequently with the manufacturer of the application.

WEB ACCESS MONITORING AND PARENTAL CONTROLS

The ability to monitor Web site requests and prevent access to objectionable content is included with many gateway devices. If you have small children, it is helpful to use these features to ensure that your youngsters don't accidentally wind up someplace scary.

Parental controls work by blocking access to objectionable sites. Block lists are updated frequently as new sites are discovered.

Secure your wireless network

If you brought home a wireless network gateway and plugged it in without setting up security, chances are that your neighbor kid has been enjoying free broadband for some time now.

By enabling wireless security protocols, you make it more difficult to see into your network—not only for the neighborhood kids, but also for anyone who happens to drive by. These protocols extend protection to your VoIP calls by ensuring that the local IP address for your TA is not known or visible to anyone who attempts to crack it.

All wireless gateways include some encryption features. If you purchased your gateway in 2005 or later, chances are that it can even stop someone from breaking the encryption. If this discussion has you heading to the store to get a new one, be sure that it supports 802.11i/WPA2 wireless encryption.

Use encryption for direct calls

Services like those provided by Vonage and BroadVoice use devices on the provider's network called *session controllers* to manage call processing. Having known endpoints for the Internet phone communication provides some assurance that you are connecting with your VoIP provider's networks. If you choose a service that directly connects users to one another, such as Free World Dialup (FWD), you need to be more careful. You may even want to encrypt your communication when using these services, because you have no idea what Internet backwaters your traffic might pass through on its way to your acquaintance. Some services have their own encryption. The Skype softphone includes its own proprietary encryption to protect the contents of your call from others.

If you are using direct calling services like these, there is no reason you cannot use additional security measures such as Internet Protocol Security (IPSec) encryption to create a virtual private network (VPN) to protect your call. When using these methods, you'll need to configure both ends of the communication. VPN connection endpoint capabilities are available as features of some Internet gateway devices. The manufacturer instructions explain how to set up and configure these features.

Avoiding SPIT

Folks who see black helicopters warn that VoIP systems might in the future be subject to spam-style attacks by mass marketers. Called *Spam over Internet Telephony (SPIT)*, this technology would lead to mass placement of advertising directly in subscriber's voice-mail boxes.

Although many providers steadfastly claim that this is not possible with their networks, theorists hold that it may yet come to pass. Whether this happens remains to be seen.

If you receive unsolicited calls, ask to be placed on the caller's Do Not Call list. Better yet, subscribe to the National Do Not Call Registry at www.donotcall.gov. If you receive messages that arrive without the phone's ringing at all, notify your provider. The provider will know whether the caller attempted to call when your phone was not available and can initiate an investigation into the possibility of a SPIT attack.

THAT'S GREAT, BUT WHAT IS SPAM?

Spam is mass unsolicited e-mailings that clutter inboxes with offers for pharmaceuticals, get-rich-quick schemes, and physique-enhancing compounds of all types. Although spam has been classified as illegal in the United States, it is extremely hard to locate the senders of these messages, and enough people fall for the claims to make it profitable for the spam purveyors.

Many tools are available to combat spam. A quick Google search for "SpyBot Search and Destroy" will find one of the best.

Learn More about VoIP Security

As security issues surrounding Internet telephony continue to evolve, a book cannot possibly keep you up to date for more than a few weeks at best. To help you find out more about what is happening with VoIP security, I have included the following resources. Use them to locate additional information about security topics and issues affecting the VoIP community.

VoIP security resources

The following Web sites and online resources follow developments in VoIP and should have information about current security issues:

Fire the Phone Company Blog (www.firethephonecompany.info)

This Web log, which I maintain, covers news and events affecting the consumer Internet phone industry.

The VoIP Wiki (www.voip-info.org/tiki-index.php)

The VoIP Wiki includes references to VoIP setup, security specifications, and new technologies.

Request for Comments Document 3329, Security Mechanism Agreement for the Session Initiation Protocol (SIP) (www.faqs.org/rfcs/rfc3329.html)

Request for Comments documents define proposed Internet standards. When ratified, they become specifications for the adoption of new practices and technologies (good bedtime reading).

VoIP security organizations

These organizations promote security awareness and describe new standards for VoIP security. These bodies include members of the community of VoIP manufacturers, VoIP providers, and users of VoIP services.

VOICE OVER IP SECURITY ALLIANCE (VOIPSA)

Loaded with very smart people, this group evaluates research and analysis of VoIP security vulnerabilities and promotes remedies for these vulnerabilities. Representatives from major VoIP manufacturers, consulting firms, and standards bodies attend regular conference calls to discuss VoIP security issues and find solutions to these issues.

To follow along with the efforts of VOIPSA, you can visit its Web site at www.voipsa.org.

INTERNET ENGINEERING TASK FORCE (IETF)

The IETF is the standards body for most Internet technologies. Its RFCs, which have the effect of creating standards for Internet communications, govern the structure of the Internet as it exists today.

VoIP, itself an Internet technology, is governed by several RFCs covering everything from the structure of VoIP packets to the signaling employed to make and break calls. As security proposals are generated by VOIPSA, they will no doubt take the form of RFCs in which the IETF becomes involved.

The IETF's Web site is at www.ietf.org.

CHAPTER EIGHT

Getting the Best Value from VoIP

In this chapter, I present some of the financial justifications for implementing Internet phone service. Some of these justifications have been known by business telecommunications executives for some time. Most corporate call centers have been using VoIP to lower costs and increase efficiency, and more than 50 percent of all new business phone lines are using IP telephony.

It's about time we bring the savings home.

IN THIS CHAPTER

The VoIP Value Equation **138**

The Value of Convergence **142**

Finding Business Value with VoIP **145**

The Bottom Line **146**

The VoIP Value Equation

Wait! Come back!

You didn't think I'd bring you this far only to drop some heavy math on you and leave, did you? And for the guy who thought he knew which equation I was talking about? Sorry!

The value of Internet phone service is much more common-sense than some equation. It is the money you will save with unlimited local and long-distance dialing, the free calls made by family members and friends to your number, and the inexpensive toll-free line you can add to your home business.

More than unlimited minutes

Sure, you have seen the "unlimited long distance" plans from the long-distance telephone companies. But how many of them can offer this *plus* local telephone service for less than $25 a month? This is where VoIP brings the value home. Let's look at the ways VoIP providers save you money on long distance.

ALL LOCAL AND LONG-DISTANCE CALLS FOR ONE PRICE

With VoIP, local and long-distance calls use the minutes in your plan. This is very similar to the way billing for cell phones is done. The main difference is the price for additional minutes. Cellular phone carriers charge various rates for overages; some charge for each block of 100 additional minutes, and others charge per minute. VoIP providers? Nada. If you choose one of the many plans available for $25 a month or less, you pay nothing for additional minutes.

Long-distance carriers have similar plans. For a minimum fee—usually around $25 a month—you get unlimited long distance. But this is on top of whatever you are paying for your local phone service. Total cost? $50 to $100 per month. You save $25 or more by switching to VoIP.

VOIP PEERS CALL FREE WITH IN-NETWORK CALLING

If your friends or family members use the same VoIP provider, in most cases they do not pay anything to call you (**Figure 8.1**). This means you can send your daughter off to college with VoIP, and she can call home all you want at no additional charge. You can even choose a simple softphone plan for about $10 per month that she can use from her dorm-room computer. Total cost for all the calls Mom wants? $10.

Free in-network calling even works for overseas calls. Get your relatives in the United Kingdom set up with VoIP, and call them for free at any time. (Just remember that it might be 4 a.m. over there when you're watching the Wimbledon-highlights show.)

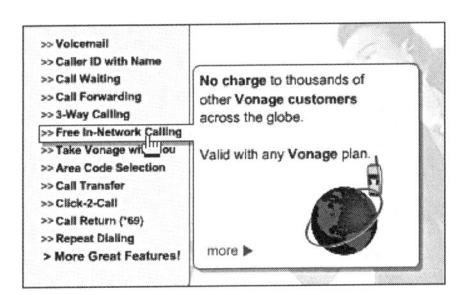

Figure 8.1 Vonage's Web site explains its In-Network Calling feature.

Virtual numbers

If your parents steadfastly refuse to make the switch, or if their home is not accessible to broadband Internet services, you can choose other options for low-cost calling. Virtual numbers are extra numbers that are added to your VoIP account. Costing $2 to $5 per month on average, they provide a phone number in another calling area that will ring on your home phone.

FAMILY AND FRIENDS CALL FREE

If some of your family members cannot use VoIP for some reason, you can add a number in their area. This lets them call you at any time as a local call. When they call this number, they pay no long-distance charges.

> **TIP**
>
> Use care when choosing the provider's rate center (city code) for this line. Make sure the rate center you choose is within the same Local Access Transport Area (LATA) as your caller. Calls within a LATA are free, but calls between LATAs (Inter-LATA) incur a toll charge. Use Google to search for "LATA map" to locate resources to help you determine whether you can use this feature.

OVERSEAS FOR FREE?

Many VoIP providers are adding the ability to obtain overseas virtual numbers. This allows you to get a number in Dublin that your aunt can call that will ring your phone in Dallas. She has to do nothing but memorize the new number.

INTERNATIONAL PLANS

Many VoIP providers offer excellent rates on international calls, connecting many parts of the world for no additional charge after the monthly fee. **Table 8.1** shows a comparison of per-minute calling rates to several international cities from New York, USA.

Toll-free numbers

For as little as $5 a month. you can add a toll-free number to your VoIP account. A toll-free number typically comes with a pool of minutes, and you are charged by the minute after the pool is exhausted. Check with your chosen provider to see whether it offers this service.

> **NOTE**
>
> Inexpensive toll-free numbers are a great benefit to small home businesses. They give you that "big business" look for an affordable fee. They are also a great way to let traveling friends and family members call you for free.

VoIP direct saves even more

If you can do without the actual telephone, you can make VoIP-to-VoIP calls on the Internet for free. There is no charge to register and use services such as Skype, Free World Dialup, Yahoo!, and MSN for VoIP calling. You can call anywhere in the world with these services.

> **TIP**
>
> If you need to call someone who has a landline phone, a service like SkypeOut costs only 1.7 euro cents per minute (about 2 cents U.S.) and is run on a prepaid basis. This is fine for occasional use. More extensive use may justify moving to an international plan with a VoIP provider.

Table 8.1 Comparing Overseas Rates per Minute (VoIP vs. Traditional Long Distance)

New York To:	AT&T International	MCI Global Connection	BroadVoice Unlimited Plus	Skype
London, United Kingdom	.10	.07	free	free
Helsinki, Finland	.10	.07	free	free
Shanghai, China	.10	.10	free	free
New Delhi, India	.28	.28	.16	free
Cape Town, South Africa	.37	.39	.10	free

The Value of Convergence

Those familiar with business-costs analysis will readily see the savings in terms of time and labor when services such as telephone, fax, and e-mail are converged. Having one way to access all these features allows employees to get more done in less time, saving the business money and increasing its ability to respond quickly to customers.

These same value statements hold true for home use. If you are able to get your online work done more quickly, you will have more time to spend with your family.

- Being able to make calls to the entire soccer team by recording your message once and having it sent to a list of phone numbers could save the busy soccer coach more than half an hour of making calls.

- Receiving an e-mail notification of a voice-mail message at work lets you know that someone attempted to reach you at home.

- Listening to your voice mail online allows you to know that this evening's committee meeting has been cancelled and you can go straight home after work.

Integrated messaging

Many VoIP services allow you to integrate e-mail and voice mail. You can receive notifications of voice-mail messages and listen to them online. Services like Free World Dialup offer integration with instant-messaging clients from Microsoft, Yahoo!, and America Online (AOL), as well as their own messaging tools. This helps users know when others are online and allows them to choose voice or text, depending on their circumstances.

INSTANT-MESSAGING CLIENTS

Microsoft Messenger and Yahoo! Messenger now have the ability to make and receive Internet calls between messaging subscribers. Yahoo! even uses technology provided by Net2Phone to allow users to call standard telephone numbers.

With these clients, you can make voice and video calls, chat, send e-mail, and search for new contacts, all within one application. For those who primarily use computers when communicating, these tools offer great value.

INITIATIVES BY MAJOR ONLINE SERVICES

Some mega Internet access providers like AOL now offer Internet phone service. This service offers the same features discussed in earlier chapters plus integration with AOL's other services.

AOL Internet Phone allows you to make and receive calls with a regular telephone. The service also offers features such as the ability to call people from your AOL contacts list, listen and respond to e-mails by phone, and receive e-mail notification of voice-mail messages.

Contact list integration

Some VoIP services offer the ability to retrieve contacts from Microsoft Outlook or other e-mail programs and to initiate calls to one of more contacts at the same time (**Figure 8.2**). You can send a message to all your friends by selecting their numbers from your contacts list. This saves you the time required to look up all those numbers and eliminates misdialing.

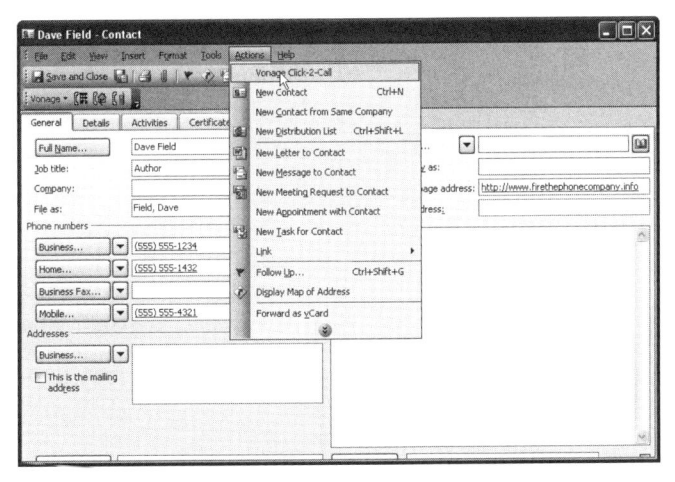

Figure 8.2 The Vonage Click-2-Call feature integrates with Microsoft Outlook and other Windows applications.

Fax over Internet

For about $10 per month, you can add a fax line to your VoIP service to send and receive fax messages from your home. For a small home business, this saves more than $20 per month in dedicated line charges, in addition to long-distance savings. Fax over Internet uses the G.711 codec to ensure good call quality. The service typically can use the second port in your TA (telephone adapter) to connect the fax machine so that you don't need additional telephone hardware. (You still need a fax machine, though.)

Multimedia communications

As VoIP services evolve, users are discovering new ways to communicate. Imagine a conference call in which you can also send instant messages to other callers to discuss strategy as the call progresses. You can also participate in calls where some participants use video and others use voice, depending on their equipment and their location (**Figure 8.3**).

Some softphone services, such as ineen.com, are using softphones to send and receive video, too (**Figure 8.4**).

Figure 8.3 Packet8 offers its VideoPhone service for about the cost of its standard VoIP offerings.

Figure 8.4 Ineen offers voice and video communications using the XTen eyeBeam softphone.

Finding Business Value with VoIP

Although this book is dedicated to consumer VoIP, the evangelist in me cannot resist telling you about all the ways you can save money with VoIP for a small business. Most large businesses have already heard the message and are rolling out Internet phone systems. As a result, experts in the Internet telephony field are in great demand right now. Installing your own Internet phone system for your small business will save you money both during installation (if you do it yourself) and during normal operation.

Business-to-business (B2B) VoIP

If you make a large number of calls to one or more business clients, explore the possibility of establishing a dedicated VoIP trunk to those clients. This can be as simple as setting up a compatible phone and dialing their Internet phones directly.

If your business partners use a more complex IP phone system, such as the Cisco Call Manager and Cisco IP phones, you might consider having one of their phones installed in your offices. Their staff can provision your connection, and you can communicate hotline style to their offices.

A telecommuter's dream

VoIP trunks can also benefit employees who spend a significant amount of time working from home. By installing a company Internet phone in your home, you can enjoy the same level of communications that you get at your desk in the office. With VoIP, it is very easy to install phones at remote locations due to the global reach of the Internet.

Essentially free for business

When businesses undertake large-scale installations of VoIP phones, they often build their own infrastructures. After the installation costs and operation, all their calls within their networks are essentially free. They can truly "fire the phone company" and become phone companies unto themselves.

The Bottom Line

This chapter is intended to help you justify Internet phone to yourself, to your significant other, or to your boss. You should be able to make a compelling argument about direct and indirect cost savings. Following is the "executive summary."

Direct savings offer most compelling reason to switch

By far the most important factor in Internet phone savings is the lower cost for basic service and long distance. Often, for the cost of a basic phone line, you can enjoy unlimited long distance as well. Features like virtual numbers and toll-free numbers let you share your savings with family members, friends, and business associates.

Accessibility + integration + convergence = ROI

Business analysts use a term called Return on Investment (ROI) to show how fast an investment will earn back its initial expense. Some of the earnings will come from direct savings on phone charges; other savings are more subtle.

Indirect savings in both time and money add up as well. By communicating more efficiently, we save time and get more work done. This gives us more time for family and friends or (gasp) to get even *more* work done.

PHONE/FAX/E-MAIL INTEGRATION

By integrating phone, fax, and e-mail, you can message contacts in the most efficient medium. Having everything in one spot lets you get the message off quickly, whether you have your system dial the phone or simply compose a fax or e-mail from within your contact manager.

"FIND ME" FEATURES FOR TRAVELING EMPLOYEES

Having a system that follows you enables others to locate you by calling a single number. This saves time and toll charges spent calling one number after another in the search for your current whereabouts.

CHAPTER NINE

Traveling with VoIP

Much has been made of the ability of VoIP telephones to work anywhere you can find broadband Internet. Suppose you are planning to try this out on your next business trip. There are a few things to consider as you make your plans.

In this chapter, I show you how to travel with VoIP. I help you make sure you bring everything you need to communicate on the road. I cover transportation and security, how to reconnect to your VoIP provider, and where to look for broadband while traveling.

IN THIS CHAPTER
Packing Your Bags **148**
Finding Broadband **152**
Connecting to the Mother Ship **159**
Travel Safely **161**

Packing Your Bags

If you throw your telephone adapter (TA) into your suitcase and go, you will probably not have a good experience with Internet phone service while on the road. Having a travel kit prepared can help you get connected and ensure that your system is ready to use wherever you are.

What to bring

In addition to your TA, you'll want to have a variety of cables and connectors, power supplies, and reference resources with you. I have taken the liberty of preparing a list that you can check off as you assemble your travel kit:

- ❏ Your TA and its power supply
- ❏ Your TA's quick-start guide
- ❏ Category 5 patch cable to connect your TA to broadband
- ❏ Your Internet gateway (if you plan to make calls while you use your computer)
- ❏ Your gateway's setup guide
- ❏ A telephone handset
- ❏ RJ-11 phone cord to connect the handset to your TA
- ❏ Softphone software (just in case)
- ❏ This book
- ❏ A padded carrying case

If you are traveling to another country, you may need power adapters for your gear (**Figure 9.1**). Ask your travel agent about power in the country to which you are traveling, and obtain the correct power adapters to allow you to use your devices there.

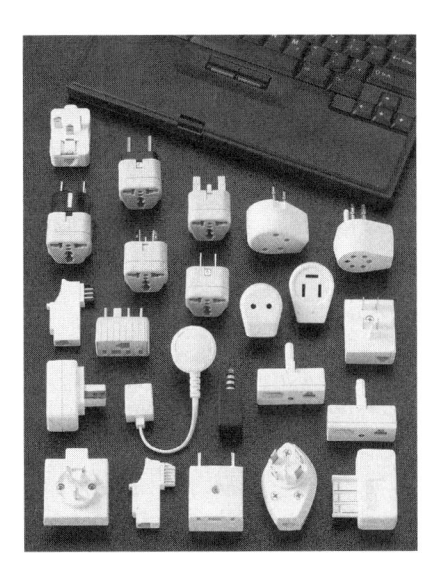

Figure 9.1 The Targus Travel Power World Pack connects your equipment to power in more than 100 countries.

If your travel destination uses 220/240 volt power systems, you may need to purchase a different power supply for your TA that can handle this voltage (**Figure 9.2**). Consult your TA's documentation to determine whether it can use 220/240 volt power. If it cannot, vendors like Targus manufacture adaptable power supplies that operate over a wide voltage range. These power supplies are typically supplied with connectors to connect with a wide range of devices.

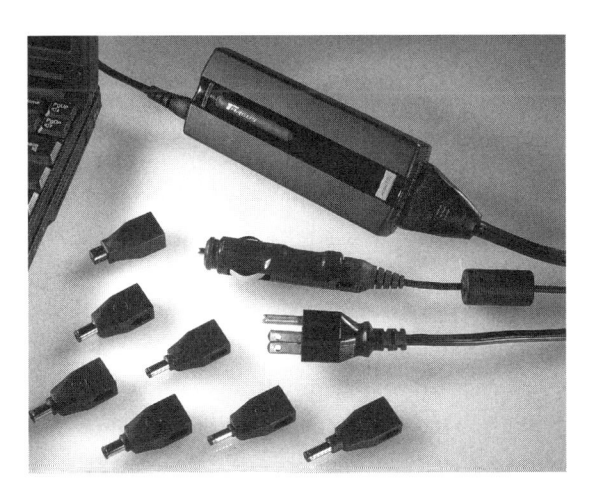

Figure 9.2 The Targus Mobile 70 Universal AC/DC Adapter operates at 100 to 230 volts and can supply power to a wide range of devices.

TIP

If you plan to carry your telephone equipment on a plane, make sure the bag you buy meets the airline's size limitations for carry-on luggage.

Protecting your gear

Travel subjects your belongings to a lot of bumps and bruises. Electronic devices are especially sensitive to being dropped on the ground, kicked, and piled under a mountain of luggage. Consider buying a travel case for your phone equipment. A padded case designed for camera equipment should be fine (**Figure 9.3**).

Figure 9.3 The CaseLogic VBS-1 camcorder bag has plenty of room (and padding) for your phone equipment.

Avoiding an inquisition

Airline security being what it is, you might expect a few questions about the contents of your telephone kit. Answer the security agent's questions politely and as completely as you can. Offer to plug in your TA to demonstrate that it is a piece of working electronic equipment. Show the manual or this book to the agent to explain what this kit is intended to accomplish. It is helpful if the bag doesn't contain anything that will raise additional concerns. Whatever you do, don't pack the children's modeling clay in the same bag!

If you don't want to deal with the likely interview at the security checkpoint, you might consider checking your kit as baggage.

Your TA is in Phoenix?!

Okay, you took my advice and checked your kit as baggage. If you are in Phoenix, you are all set. If not, you might think your chances of using your phone on this trip are pretty low.

Don't despair.

Call your VoIP provider's customer-service folks, and ask if you can use a softphone while your TA is out of the state. You might have to pay a small fee to activate a softphone, but it will probably be less than what you would pay for a few minutes of calls from a hotel phone.

If you are not traveling with a laptop, you might be out of luck unless you have done some careful planning. Some users of softphone applications have been able to run them on Internet café computers. Some softphones, like Skype's, will run from a single program file that can be stored on a keychain storage drive (**Figure 9.4**). Be sure to test this solution before leaving home to make sure you know how to locate and run your softphone from your drive.

Figure 9.4 These USB flash drives from Haimei Electronics attach to your keychain and have plenty of room for your softphone.

Finding Broadband

An Internet phone system really isn't very much use without an Internet connection. If you are a road warrior, especially if you travel with notebook computers, you are familiar with locating Internet access points. You know, for example, that many coffee shops offer wireless Internet hotspots and wired network jacks. You are also familiar with the process for obtaining high-speed Internet access in hotels, convention centers, and airport terminals.

For those who do not have this experience, I cover a few ways to locate and use Internet access points while you are on the road.

Hotspots

Internet hotspots are all the rage today. Many companies are making good money providing this service to travelers in airports and customers of restaurants, coffee shops, and malls.

Let's take a look at a few ways you can locate a hotspot.

AIRPORTS

Most large airports offer Internet access to travelers. Often, you can obtain information about available hotspots by visiting an information desk or simply by powering up your notebook computer and seeing whose hotspot home page pops up when you open your Web browser.

Because you might feel a bit self-conscious unpacking all your Internet phone gear in a busy airport terminal, you may opt for a softphone in this environment.

COFFEE SHOPS

The most likely places to find an Internet hotspot, coffee shops have a reputation as being places to connect and communicate. Some provide free access; others use fee-based hotspot solutions provided by vendors like T-Mobile. Look for a hotspot sign near the entrance to see which of these options the coffee shop provides.

Like airports, coffee shops are probably best suited to softphones.

> **TIP**
>
> For a much more in-depth review of Internet connectivity options while you travel, Peachpit has a great book titled *Global Mobile: Connecting without Walls, Wires, or Borders*. It is written by Fred Johnson, former Yahoo! executive and current Apple product manager. This book presents great ideas for mobile connectivity for both Windows and Mac computers. I highly recommend picking up a copy.

SHOPPING MALLS

Many shopping malls are beginning to offer public hotspots to give their patrons better communication abilities. Look for these near food courts or other large gathering places. Coffee shops in malls are a sure bet.

HOTSPOT LOCATORS

Many hotspot locators are available on the Internet (**Figure 9.5**). These tools let you enter information about the area you are searching and return a list of public hotspots that you can use in that area.

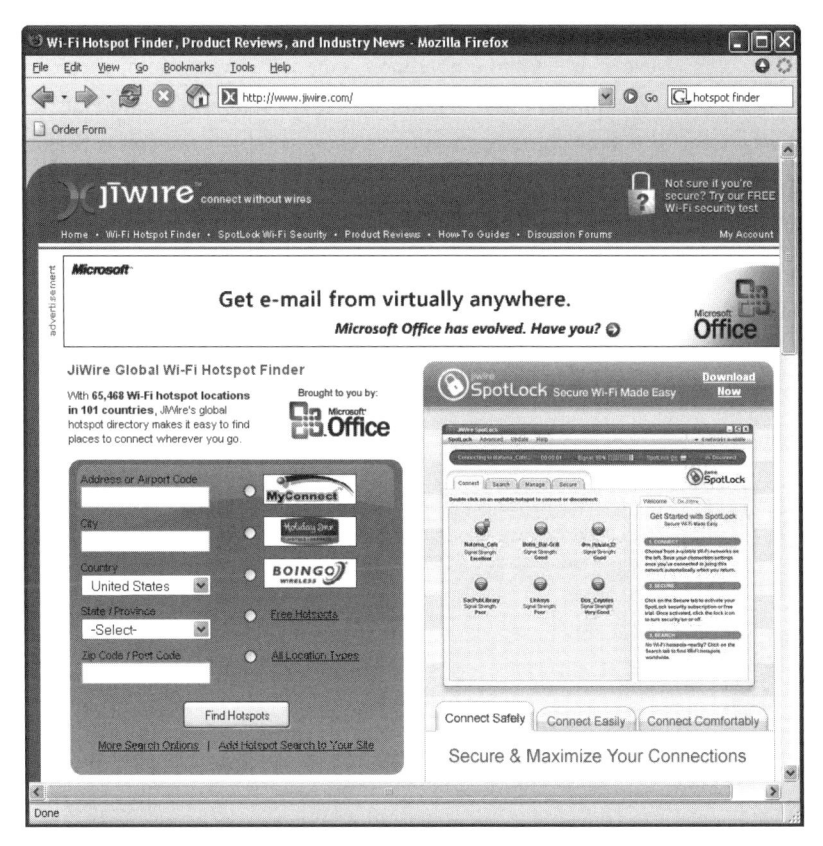

Figure 9.5 The JiWire Global Wi-Fi Hotspot Finder allows you to list all known public hotspots in a given area.

These locators are excellent at locating hotspots that you might not otherwise know about. The only drawback is that you must already be online to do the search. Searching before you leave home is an excellent way to be prepared to use these services when you arrive at your destination.

Hotels

Hotels and conference centers often offer a mixture of wired and wireless Internet options. Many offer wired high-speed Internet in guest rooms and wireless hotspots in public meeting areas. Before you travel, call ahead to your hotel to find out exactly which options it offers and what you will need to bring along to get your systems connected.

If you plan to use your TA and a notebook computer in your room, consider bringing along a compact Internet gateway (**Figure 9.6**), which offers all the features of a larger gateway in a more compact size. Connection to the hotel's network is similar to your setup at home; you just need to get the appropriate addressing and gateway settings from the hotel staff.

If you plan to stay at your hotel for some time, setting up your system like you do at home will allow you to use the full capabilities of your VoIP service. In addition, having a familiar telecommunications setup will help you be more productive and is worth the extra effort that it takes to bring it on the trip.

Figure 9.6 Linksys makes the WRT54GC compact gateway especially for travelers and those with limited desk space in their home office.

Finding Broadband **CHAPTER NINE** 155

Business centers

Many hotels and conference centers offer business-center services where you can use networked computers, copiers, faxes, and printers (**Figure 9.7**). Many of these centers also offer connections for your own equipment. If you do not have high-speed Internet in your room, you can use these facilities to connect and communicate from your hotel.

Figure 9.7 The business center at the Grand Hotel Minneapolis

Wireless cities

Many cities are undertaking wireless Internet initiatives to provide their citizens affordable access to broadband Internet. Cities like Grand Haven, Michigan, and Chaska, Minnesota, have installed systems that let citizens connect to a citywide wireless network with Internet access (**Figure 9.8**). The cost of these connections is much below that offered by cable and DSL Internet providers because of the large volume of users who share the cost of the system.

If you are interested in wireless Internet in your community, attend a city-council meeting or inquire of city staff whether they have plans to install such a network. If they do not, you might have to be the one to make it happen in your community.

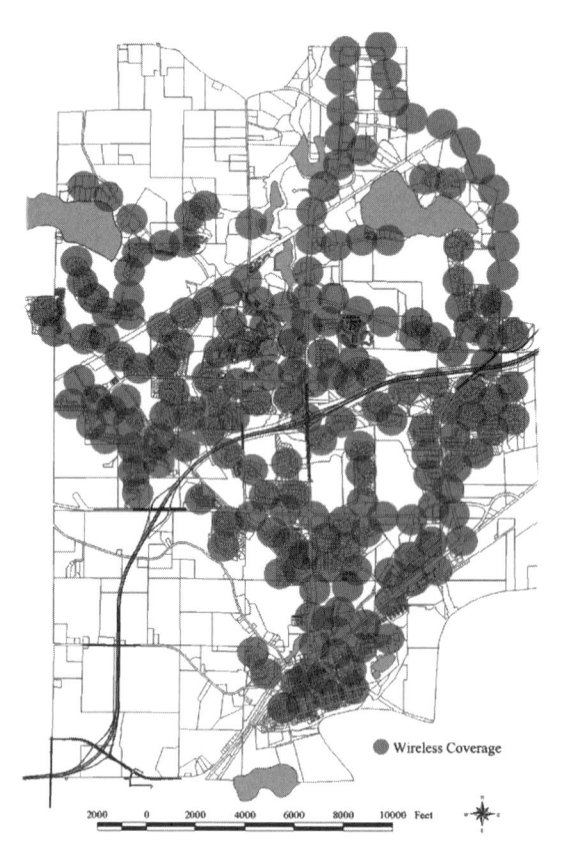

Figure 9.8 Coverage map for Chaska.net in Chaska, Minnesota

Finding Broadband **CHAPTER NINE** 157

Using wireless Internet

"But my TA needs a wired connection!" you exclaim.

You're absolutely right.

There are a few tricks, however, to getting connected to a wireless network.

WIRELESS NETWORK BRIDGES

One way to connect to a wireless network is to find a way to enable your equipment to communicate wirelessly. You can accomplish this task with a device called a *wireless Ethernet bridge* (**Figure 9.9**). This device connects to a wired network, a computer, or a TA and transmits and receives data across the wireless network.

To connect your TA to the wireless network, complete the instructions provided in the bridge's quick-start guide. When the bridge is online, connect and power up your TA. It should locate your provider and be available for calls within a few minutes.

Figure 9.9 The Linksys WET54GS5 connects up to five wired network devices to a wireless network.

> **NOTE**
>
> The computer and networking press has published many reports lately about the existence of "open" wireless networks. Groups of computer hobbyists travel the country, mapping these unprotected wireless networks via a practice called *wardriving*. Most wardrivers would never consider actually using the resources of these networks; rather, they locate them as a hobby. You should never attempt to connect to these networks. Use of a computer or network without the owner's permission is against the law and can land you in jail.

WIRELESS PHONES

Many manufacturers are now producing phones that are designed to connect to wireless networks and make Internet calls (**Figure 9.10**). These phones include wireless network transceivers along with the functionality of a TA, all in a package about the size of a cell phone. As you will see in the next chapter, there are even devices coming onto the market that will function as cell phones when wireless Internet is not available.

Wireless phones do have their limitations. Hotspot operators must make a provision in their networks for these devices. Many hotspots require some form of authentication that verifies your identity before they will allow you to use the network, but these phones have no way to accomplish this. Open hotspots, such as those in many airports and convention centers, allow these phones to connect and call without any problem.

As wireless phones gain popularity, more hotspots will begin to support them, making them more useful as an alternative to cell phones or softphones.

Figure 9.10 The Cisco 7920 Wireless IP phone

Connecting to the Mother Ship

You've made it to your hotel, have all your equipment, and have located the broadband jack in your room.

Now what?

In this section, I summarize the steps to take to get your system connected and working with your VoIP service.

Connecting your TA

Your TA should work exactly like it does at home. If you have connected it using the default setup from your VoIP provider, it should be a "plug and dial" hookup for you. If you have modified the device settings or set a fixed IP address to make it work with your home network, you might have to configure it to obtain an address from the hotel network. (To accomplish that task, use the voice-response menus built into your TA.) Consult the manufacturer's instructions if you have any questions about how to access these menus on your TA.

If you have been using your TA with an Internet gateway device, you might consider bring the gateway along to simplify things. You will most likely need to use the setup guide for your gateway to get it communicating with the hotel's network.

You did bring a handset, didn't you?

After your TA is online, just plug in your handset and start making calls.

If you have forgotten your handset, do not try connecting the hotel phone to your TA. Many hotel phones are designed to operate on different types of phone systems and would not be compatible with your TA; some might even damage your TA's circuitry.

If you don't have a handset, consider using a softphone with your notebook computer—the topic of the next section.

TIP

Use the quick-start guide included with your TA for a quick way to set up and get online on the road. These instructions will work for most of the connections you find. Call your VoIP provider if you still need assistance.

Leaving the TA at home (or Phoenix)

Many travelers opt not to bring their TA on the road; they bring their notebook computer and use a VoIP softphone instead. Most VoIP service providers offer softphone options for a small fee; these options can give you excellent mobility on the road.

BROADBAND PHONE ON THE GO

Most major broadband phone companies offer softphone options. Phones like the XTen X-PRO softphone work with several VoIP providers when you add a softphone line to your service (**Figure 9.11**). These options are a great deal for the extra mobility you will receive. You can use the softphone anywhere your notebook computer can get a high-speed connection, and you do not have to reconfigure the softphone each time you try to use it in a new location.

Figure 9.11 The XTen X-Pro softphone configured for Vonage's SoftPhone service

HAVE SKYPE, WILL TRAVEL

If you use free services like Skype and Free World Dialup, you already have the setup you need to communicate on the road. Just find the Internet, and start calling. You will have the same tools you use at home to make and receive calls.

Travel Safely

Finally, let's look at a few things you should consider when traveling to make your journey a safe one. Just because you are on vacation doesn't mean that the hackers are as well. You can take a few common-sense steps to make sure you can use your equipment safely while on the road.

Don't forget security

If you read the newspaper, watch television, or listen to the radio, you have read/seen/heard reports about Internet viruses, worms, spam, phishing, and so on. You need to take the same precautions on the road against these threats that you would take at home.

WIRELESS SECURITY

For all intents and purposes, a wireless network is like an old party-line telephone; everyone who has access to the network can hear what everyone else is saying. If you are planning to use your systems for sensitive communications, consider this fact, and take appropriate measures to ensure that your communications are protected. These measures may include using encrypted softphones (like the kind provided by Skype) or virtual private networks that connect you to a trusted network before you initiate your call.

INTERNET SECURITY

As a minimum, install a good personal firewall and antivirus program on your notebook computer to protect your system whenever you are connected to the Internet.

Beyond that, I cannot possibly do this important topic justice in these pages. If security is important to you, please pick up a book that deals with Internet security to learn how to make your systems secure. There are several good choices—some written by me and some written by other Peachpit authors. Check your local bookstore for one that speaks to your level of interest and skill with this topic.

> **NOTE**
>
> Virtual private networks and encryption are advanced security technologies; operating them correctly requires additional knowledge and configuration. If you do not have these resources set up already, consult a good book on Internet security for advice about setup and operation.

Register your 911 service

Your VoIP provider's 911 service is fixed to the location you provided when you last configured 911. During your travels, if you plan to be in one location for any length of time, register your new location with your provider's 911 service. You can usually do this on the provider's Web site, and the process takes only a few minutes.

CHAPTER TEN

VoIP into the Future

This is the part of the book where we put on our funny glasses and high collars, and look ahead to the bright future of technology. Though many forecasts have very little hope of actually seeing the ozone-depleted light of some future day, the predictions I present here are for VoIP technologies that are quite likely to be produced. Many are actually in trials or in limited availability right now and expected to be in wide release soon.

> **IN THIS CHAPTER**
> Internet (Video)Phone 164
> (More) Convergence 167
> Wireless VoIP 171
> Cellular and Wireless VoIP Combo Phones 173

Internet (Video)Phone

If you have seen science-fiction movies at any time since about 1950, you have no doubt seen a videophone. Various flavors of videophone have been produced over the years. They have almost always been very expensive and impossible to use if there wasn't an exact replica of your phone on the other end of the line. Although the interoperability angle hasn't quite been solved yet, I am happy to report that some videophones have broken the $300 barrier.

Available today

A number of videophones are now available that use VoIP technologies for voice and video transmission. Some vendors, such as Packet8, are already offering hardware videophone solutions to customers at monthly rates competitive with those of voice-only services.

HARDWARE VIDEO PHONES

The Packet8 videophone has starred in shows such as "Alias," "24," and "Law & Order: Special Victims Unit" (**Figure 10.1**). Even with all its fame, the actual phone remains quite accessible and functional. At competitive monthly rates, this phone offers full-motion video between two callers and can be used to transmit prerecorded video via a video input jack.

Figure 10.1 The Packet8 videophone

Internet (Video)Phone   CHAPTER TEN   165

The Motorola Ojo videophone looks almost otherworldly by comparison and sports a detachable cordless handset (**Figure 10.2**). While it hasn't had the same level of prime-time media exposure, it is reported to be selling well and is getting good reviews. It is more expensive (about $500 more) than the Packet8 phone but is designed to be compatible with future videophones from other manufacturers.

Figure 10.2 The Motorola Ojo videophone is compatible with other videophone devices.

VIDEO SOFTPHONES

For those of you who don't mind sitting at the PC when calling, you can make use of videophone software from Dialcom and ineen. These video softphones are inexpensive to set up and allow you to make calls at very reasonable rate.

Dialcom's Spontania Video4Skype plug-in for the free Skype VoIP service offers you the ability to call Skype users and converse voice-only or with video (**Figure 10.3**). Available free from www.video4skype.com, this plug-in works on both Windows 2000 and Windows XP computers.

Figure 10.3 Video4Skype enables free videophone calls over the Skype service.

Ineen is a video softphone built on the XTen eyeBeam development platform (**Figure 10.4**). Usable as a standard VoIP softphone, this phone also works with the ineen VoIP videophone service. This softphone can be used with Windows and Mac computers and with Windows Mobile devices. Linux versions are in the works.

Figure 10.4 The ineen video softphone enables multiple concurrent videophone calls over the ineen network.

Coming soon

Even on "Star Trek," away teams were restricted to using voice-only technology. How cool would it have been for Captain Kirk to have whipped out a pocket videophone?

Well, we probably won't have to wait for the 24th century for the pleasure of seeing loved ones while away from the house. Some manufacturers are now testing wireless videophones that will use VoIP technology to transmit video. If you think cell phones cause accidents, just wait until some poor Joe gets a look at what his wife is packing for their weekend trip!

Bam!

(More) Convergence

I have discussed some of the converged features available today with VoIP technologies, especially those available with softphones. Not content to rest on their laurels, the purveyors of this converged nirvana are working diligently to offer even more features and functionality.

Unified softphones

Softphones offer some of the most potential for dramatically converged systems. Being software, these devices are inherently flexible and can be plugged into larger systems to offer features we can only imagine today.

IM CONVERGENCE

The pulver.Communicator is a good example of the convergence coming to this area (**Figure 10.5**). This application is already capable of managing contacts and messaging among Skype, MSN, Yahoo!, AOL, and ICQ. It can

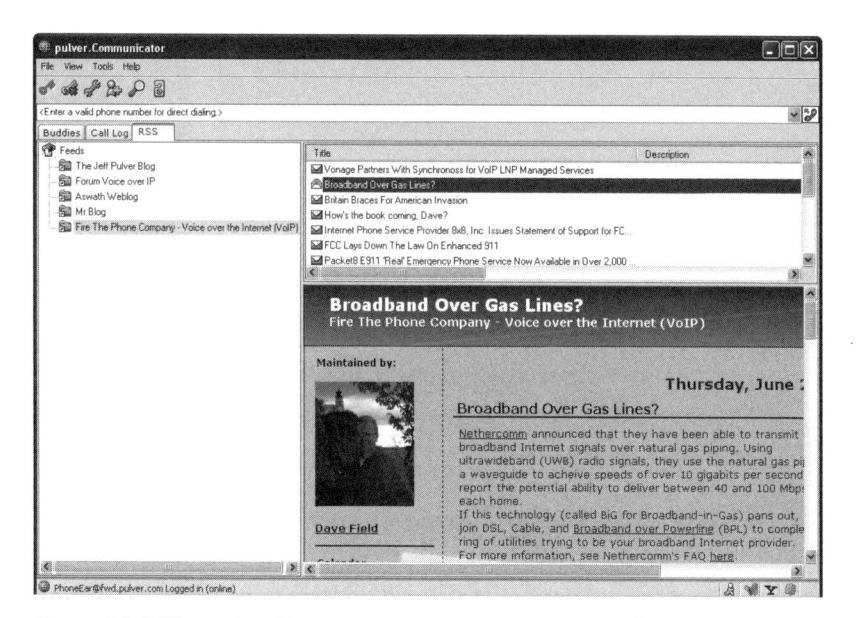

Figure 10.5 The pulver.Communicator integrates many different messaging services.

also manage news feeds from blogs and online news sites by using Really Simple Syndication (RSS), a protocol for publishing information about new articles. As products in this area mature, look for tools that integrate voice calling, video calling, e-mail, voice mail, video mail, and instant messaging in one universal communications tool.

REMOTE PRESENTATION AND REMOTE CONTROL

Products like Microsoft NetMeeting have been offering remote presentation and control for a number of years now. Other companies, such as WebEx and Go2MyPC.com, are offering products in this area as well (**Figure 10.6**). As these products integrate VoIP functionality, expect to see the equivalent of video/voice conference calls with remote control and whiteboard sharing.

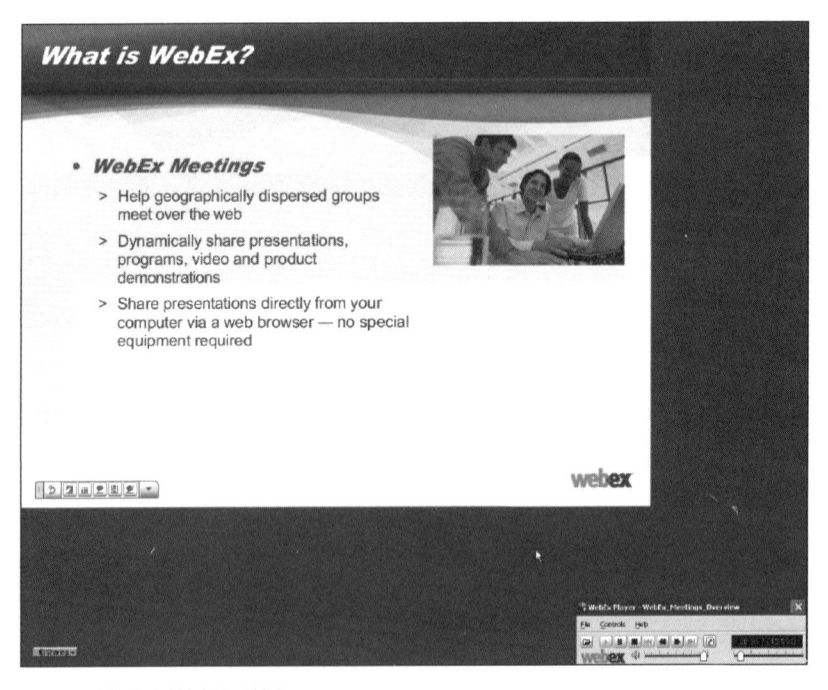

Figure 10.6 A WebEx Web presentation

Business convergence

Businesses using IP telephone systems can use the features of IP phones to integrate their business systems with their phone systems. Having the ability to initiate calls from within a contact manager or sales application not only makes it easier to initiate calls, but also eliminates the potential for misdialed numbers.

Other efficiencies are being realized in call-center applications that bring up a customer's profile as that number is being autodialed. Help-desk operators are able to get up-to-date information on a client's computer configuration as the system looks up customer data from caller ID information fed into the system by the incoming VoIP call. As a result, they can quickly tell whether there are performance issues related to insufficient hardware.

MICROSOFT OUTLOOK

Many VoIP providers offer integration with Microsoft Outlook. This continues on the business side of VoIP, with business phone systems offering similar integration. Calls can be initiated directly from Outlook and taken by softphone or VoIP desk phone. Voice mails can be viewed as e-mail and answered by e-mail or by phone.

CUSTOM INTEGRATION SOLUTIONS

As programmers get a good look at the capabilities of IP phones, they are designing custom applications that use the features of this medium (**Figure 10.7**). This integration is becoming evident in revolutionary new products and systems that improve business competitiveness and profitability (hint: CEOs love those buzzwords).

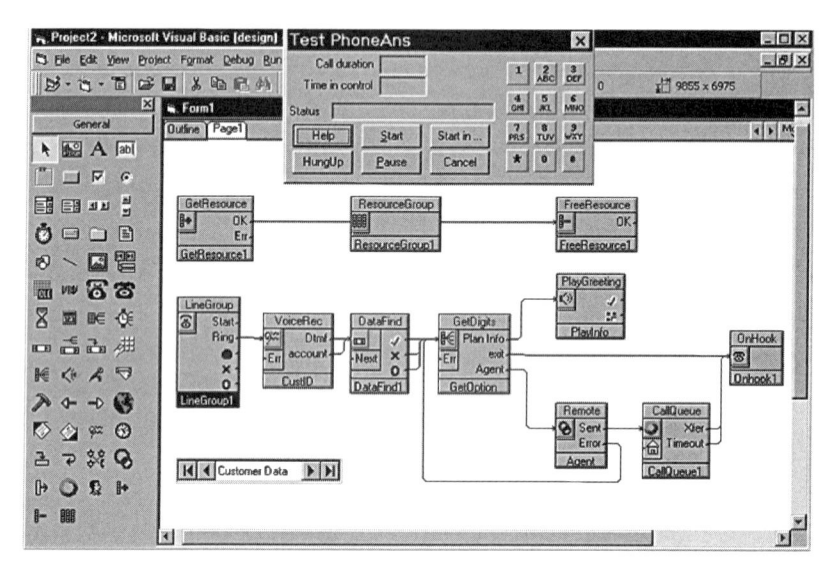

Figure 10.7 VBVoice from Pronexus allows operators to build custom interactive voice response systems by using VoIP technologies.

Wireless VoIP

Wireless networking, often called *Wi-Fi* (for **W**ireless **Fi**delity), is becoming more widespread every day. In addition to the municipalities mentioned in Chapter 9 that have undertaken to blanket their areas with wireless Internet, some cities are taking the extra step of providing VoIP service over the same wireless infrastructure. Called *Voice over Wi-Fi (VoWi-Fi)*, this service allows callers to use wireless VoIP phones at any location within the city's coverage area.

Wi-Fi VoIP phones

Several manufacturers of VoIP phones are currently producing phones that communicate over a Wi-Fi network (**Figure 10.8**). Earlier chapters discussed these phones but not the result of this development, which allows a subscriber to walk out of the house, get in the car, and drive to work without ever hanging up the phone.

AVAILABLE TODAY

Rio Rancho, New Mexico, has completed the initial stages of a citywide wireless network and has included VoIP telephone coverage as well. Working with partners Azulstar, Ecuity, and Meru Networks, the city offers unlimited stationary and mobile VoIP calling for $29.99 per month. Add $19.95 for wireless Internet, and you have total connectivity for less than $50!

Figure 10.8 The Cisco 7920 Wi-Fi phone

COMING SOON

Wireless initiatives are hatching all over. Minneapolis is planning a Wi-Fi network to allow city staff, police, and residents to build a digital community. New York City, Philadelphia, and Las Vegas are in various stages of planning for their own downtown networks.

Subscribers to these networks will have ubiquitous access to VoIP services with VoWi-Fi phones and TAs (telephone adapters) connected to wireless Ethernet bridges.

WiMax VoIP phones

WiMax is a new wireless networking initiative that is not yet ratified by the standards organizations but shows the ability to cover longer distances. Some access providers are already planning municipal networks using pre-WiMax devices. Networks using WiMax will be able to use fewer nodes to cover the same area.

No WiMax phones are available as of the writing of this book, but you can be assured that they are on the drawing board.

Cellular and Wireless VoIP Combo Phones

In the classic vein of being all things to all people, enter the cellular/VoWi-Fi phone. Some of these phones are being designed to use VoWi-Fi offerings from established VoIP providers; others will simply use Wi-Fi for Internet access to the Skype network.

i-mate PDA2/PDA2k

Called a *smartphone*, the i-mate PDA2 series of phones are GSM-band cellular phones that run the Microsoft Windows Mobile operating system (**Figure 10.9**). They also include the ability to communicate over wireless networks, enabling applications like Skype to be used for VoIP calling over the wireless network.

> **NOTE**
>
> Although this device allows users to make calls over cellular and VoIP, those features have not been integrated for seamless handoffs. You cannot pass VoIP calls on to cellular when you leave the wireless coverage area, so you will need to redial those calls if you want to take them on the road.

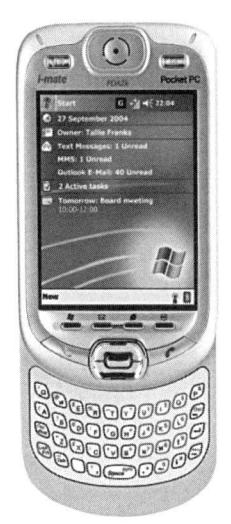

Figure 10.9 The i-mate PDA2k smartphone

Motorola CN620

Enter Motorola! Being involved with VoWi-Fi and cellular phones from the beginning, Motorola, the world's No. 3 handset maker, has been working on phones that pass cellular calls to VoIP whenever they encounter Wi-Fi networks. The CN620 is the fruition of that effort (**Figure 10.10**). Able to initiate calls over cellular or Wi-Fi, the phone also includes corporate-style extension dialing and Push to Talk (PTT) features that offer person-to-person, radio-style communications. It can hand off from Wi-Fi to cellular and back seamlessly, allowing users to make and receive calls anywhere, maintaining contact by the most economical method currently available at their location.

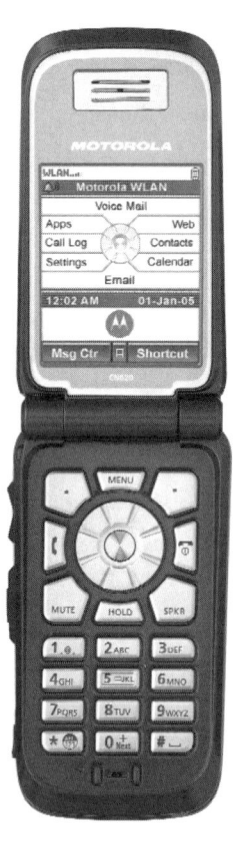

Figure 10.10 Motorola's CN620 gives you best-rate calls anywhere you go.

Index

Numbers

802.11i security, 129
911 services, 21-22
    activating, 83-86
    alternatives to, 86
    availability of, 31
    enhanced (E-911), 85
    problem resolution, 85-86
    registering for, 83, 84
    testing, 83-85
    travel issues, 86, 162

A

activating VoIP service, 80-82
    See also VoIP services
additional-line options, 93
Advanced Encryption Standard (AES), 130
airport hotspots, 152
Allen Tel AT173 modular adapter, 71, 76, 121
AOL Internet Phone, 143

B

bandwidth, 44-47
    addressing issues with, 46-47
    alternative codecs and, 106-107
    speed tests of, 46, 47, 100
    upgrading, 102
    VoIP requirements for, 45
blended services, 94
bot attacks, 128-129
bottlenecks, 45
bring your own device (BYOD), 34, 35, 96
Broadband Reports, 19, 123
BroadVoice, 96
business centers, 155
business convergence, 169-170
business-to-business (B2B) VoIP, 145

C

cable companies, 24-26
    cable outages and, 25
    evaluating for VoIP, 24-25
    service availability, 25-26
    VoIP installation by, 67-68
cables, 70
call forwarding, 90-91, 123
call hunting, 91
calling features, 30, 88-93
    call forwarding, 90-91
    call hunting, 91
    fallback number, 92
    simultaneous-ring service, 91, 94
    voice mail, 89-90
cellular/VoWi-Fi phones, 173-174
Click-2-Call feature, 94
codecs, VoIP, 7-8, 102, 106-107
coffee shop hotspots, 152
configuration issues, 112-117
    gateway configuration, 112-116
    Internet address configuration, 112-113
    MAC spoofing, 114
    port-range forwarding, 115-116
    PPPoE settings, 113
    TA configuration, 116-117
connection issues, 106-111
    bandwidth problems, 106-109
    intermittent connection loss, 110-111
    unstable connection, 111
connectors, 71
contact list integration, 143

convergence features
    businesses and, 169–170
    future trends in, 167–169
    value of, 142–144
cordless phones, 75–76
cost controls. *See* financial benefits
custom integration solutions, 170

D

demarcation point, 42, 43, 50, 70
DHCP (Dynamic Host Configuration Protocol), 4, 112
dial tone problems, 120
direct trunking, 22
distribution panel, 42, 43, 68
distribution system, 69–76
    cable providers, 68
    cordless phone, 75–76
    TA connections, 71–74
D-Link DVG-1120, 56
DNS (Domain Naming System), 4
DSL services, 20, 48

E

eavesdropping, 127
encryption, 130, 133, 161
enhanced 911 (E-911), 85

F

fallback number, 92
fax services, 93, 144
Federal Communications Commission (FCC), 21, 85
financial benefits, 137–146
    business value, 145
    convergence value, 142–144
    free services, 141
    in-network calling, 139
    international calls, 140, 141
    summary of, 146
    toll-free numbers, 140
    unlimited minutes, 138–139
    virtual numbers, 139–140
"find me" services, 90–91, 146
Fire the Phone Company blog, 123, 135
firewalls, 132
future trends, 163–174
    cellular/VoWi-Fi phones, 173–174
    convergence features, 167–171
    videophones, 164–165
    wireless VoIP, 171–172

G

G.711 codec, 7, 47, 102, 144
G.723.1 codec, 8
G.726 codec, 8, 102
G.729 codec, 8, 102
gateways, 12
    configuration issues, 112–116
    connecting TAs to, 55
    important features of, 54
    Internet settings configuration, 62–63
    managing QOS settings for, 107–109
    network configuration and, 48–50, 61–62
    security issues and, 131–132
    TAs combined with, 60–67, 109
    wired versus wireless, 51
Global Mobile: Connecting without Walls, Wires, or Borders (Johnson), 152

H

H.323 protocols, 6, 7
hardware problems, 117–121
    home wiring issues, 118–121
    TA failure, 117–118
hardware videophones, 164–165
headphone installation, 69

home wiring issues, 118–121
hosts, 5
hotel Internet options, 154
hotspot locators, 153

I

IAX (Inter-Asterisk eXchange), 6
i-mate PDA2k smartphones, 173
ineen video softphone, 166
infrastructure assessment, 39–51
in-network calling, 139
installation assistance, 36
instant messaging, 142–143
integrated messaging, 142–143
intermittent connection loss, 110–111
international calls, 140
International Engineering Task Force (IETF), 16, 136
International Telecommunication Union (ITU-T), 16
Internet
    configuring settings for, 62–63
    purchasing/activating VoIP via, 78
    service outages, 123
    testing connections to, 64–66
    wireless, 156–158
Internet access providers, 26–27
    evaluating for VoIP, 26
    service availability, 27
    VoIP provider list, 27
Internet bots, 128–129
Internet hotspots, 152–154
Internet phones
    development of, 2–3
    devices used for, 8–12
    protocols and codecs, 3–8
    See also VoIP
Internet Protocol (IP), 110
Internet Protocol Security (IPSec), 133
Internet security, 161
IP addresses, 5, 112–113, 117

J

JiWire Global Wi-Fi Hotspot Finder, 153

K

Keep Alive settings, 111

L

line tester, 120
Local Access Transport Areas (LATAs), 140
local number availability, 31
local number portability (LNP), 20–21, 86–87

M

MAC (Media Access Control) addresses, 81, 82
MAC spoofing, 114
Macintosh computers, 28
Megaco/MGCP (Media Gateway Control Protocol), 6
Microsoft Outlook, 169
MiNet protocol, 6
Motorola CN620 phone, 174
Motorola Ojo videophone, 165
multimedia communications, 144

N

National Do Not Call Registry, 134
network address translation (NAT), 132
network interface unit (NIU), 42, 67, 68
networks
    assessing, 39–40, 41
    preparing, 54–56
    reconfiguring, 48–50
    securing, 126
911 services, 21–22
    activating, 83–86
    alternatives to, 86

availability of, 31
enhanced (E-911), 85
problem resolution, 85–86
registering for, 83, 84
testing, 83–85
travel issues, 86, 162

O

online services, 143
organizations
    VoIP security, 135–136
    VoIP standards, 16
outages, 121–123
    power, 122–123
    service, 123
Outlook program, 169

P

Packet8 videophone, 164
packet loss, 110
packets, 3, 5
parental controls, 132
Pathping utility, 65–66
phone companies, 22–24
    evaluating for VoIP, 23
    service availability, 24
    VoIP provider list, 23
phone system
    accessing, 42
    demarcation point, 42, 43
    distribution panel, 42, 43
    network sketch, 39–40, 41
ping utility, 5, 64–65
planning for VoIP, 37–52
    bandwidth issues, 44–47
    demarcation issues, 42, 43, 50
    distribution issues, 43, 51
    DSL service loss, 48
    network configuration, 39–40, 41, 48–50

phone configuration, 40, 41, 42–43
    reasons for, 38
Point to Point Protocol over Ethernet (PPPoE)
  settings, 110–111, 113
port forwarding, 132
Portland Pattern Repository Wiki, 16
port-range forwarding, 115–116
ports, 115
power issues
    international travel and, 148–149
    power outages and, 122–123
    TA failure and, 118
preactivated devices, 36
problems and solutions. *See* troubleshooting
protocols
    Internet, 3–4
    VoIP, 3, 4–6
providers of VoIP. *See* VoIP providers
provisioning, 45
public safety answering point (PSAP), 83
pulver.Communicator, 167–168
purchase options, 78–79
pure VoIP providers, 18–21
    blocking problems, 21
    evaluating, 18–19
    list of major, 19
    local number portability, 20–21
    service availability, 19–20
Push to Talk (PTT) features, 174

Q

quality of service (QoS), 44
    management, 107–109
    settings, 102, 107–109

R

Really Simple Syndication (RSS), 168
Realtime Transport Protocol (RTP), 6
remote presentation, 168

Request for Comments documents, 135
resources on VoIP, 15–16
    security issues, 135
    troubleshooting issues, 123
retail purchase/activation, 78
Return on Investment (ROI), 146
ring booster, 119
ring voltages, 59, 119
Ringer Equivalence Number (REN), 119
ringer-load issues, 119
RJ-11 line cords, 70
round-trip time (RTT), 47
route, 5
routers, 5, 12
    See also gateways

S

SCCP (Skinny Client Control Protocol), 6
security issues, 125–136
    bot attacks, 127–129
    eavesdropping, 127
    encryption, 130, 133
    gateways, 131–132
    Internet security, 161
    network intruders, 126
    organizations dealing with, 135–136
    resources on, 135
    risk analysis, 131
    spam-style attacks, 134
    stealing minutes, 129
    travel considerations, 161
    wireless networks, 129–130, 133, 161
servers, 5
service plans, 33–34
service providers. See VoIP providers
service setup. See VoIP services
session controllers, 133
session protocols, 5–6
shopping mall hotspots, 153
simultaneous-ring service, 91, 94

single-line service, 72
SIP (Session Initiation Protocol), 6, 7
SIP phones, 9–10, 11
Skype softphone service, 97–100
    installing and configuring, 97–99
    proprietary encryption, 133
    traveling using, 160
    unified communications capability, 100
    videophone plug-in, 165
smartphones, 173
sockets, 115
softphones, 10, 11, 27–29
    accessory installation, 68–69
    considerations for using, 28
    evaluating providers of, 29
    installing and configuring, 97–100
    service availability, 29
    service options, 94–96
    traveling using, 160
    unified, 167–168
    video, 165–166
    VoIP provider list, 29
spam, 134
Spam over Internet Telephony (SPIT), 134
starter kits, 34, 35

T

tapping phones, 127
TCP/IP (Transmission Control Protocol/Internet Protocol), 4
telecommuters, 145
telephone adapters (TAs), 12
    activation of, 80–81
    configuration issues, 116–117
    connecting to gateways, 55
    distribution system and, 71–74
    failure of, 117–118
    gateways combined with, 60–67, 109
    installation procedure, 57–58
    placing outside gateways, 56

safety concerns, 59
troubleshooting, 58
telephone settings, 66
testing procedures
    bandwidth, 46, 47, 100
    Internet connections, 64-66
    911 services, 83-85
    voice-quality, 101
transport protocols, 6
traveling with VoIP, 147-162
    airline security and, 150
    business centers and, 155
    connection issues and, 159-160
    hotel-based Internet and, 154
    Internet hotspots and, 152-154
    911 services and, 86, 162
    packing a travel kit, 148-149
    protecting your gear, 150
    security issues and, 161
    softphone options, 160
    wireless Internet and, 156-158
troubleshooting, 105-123
    configuration issues, 112-117
    connection issues, 106-111
    hardware problems, 117-121
    outages, 121-123
    resources on, 123
two-line service, 72, 73, 74, 121

U

UDP (User Datagram Protocol), 4
unified softphones, 167-168
uninterruptible power supply (UPS), 122
unlimited minutes, 138-139
unstable connections, 111
URL (Uniform Resource Locator), 5
USB flash drives, 151
USB handsets, 10, 68-69

V

Video4Skype plug-in, 165
videophones, 164-166
    hardware videophones, 154-155
    video softphones, 165-166
virtual numbers, 18, 31, 139-140
virtual private networks (VPNs), 133, 161
voice mail, 89-90
Voice over IP Security Alliance (VOIPSA), 136
Voice over Wi-Fi (VoWi-Fi), 171-172
voice-quality testing, 101
voice-response menu, 117
VoIP
    bandwidth, 44-47
    codecs, 7-8, 102
    development of, 2-3
    future of, 163-174
    how it works, 13-15
    protocols, 3, 4-6
    resources, 15-16, 123
    security, 125-136
    standards, 16
    troubleshooting, 105-123
    wireless, 171-172
VoIP devices, 8-12
    BYOD option, 34, 35
    preactivated, 36
    routers/gateways, 12
    SIP phones, 9-10, 11
    softphones, 10, 11
    starter kits, 34, 35
    telephone adapters, 12
VoIP providers, 18-36
    cable companies, 24-26
    criteria for evaluating, 30-32
    equipment options, 34-36
    installation assistance, 36
    Internet access companies, 26-27
    911 services and, 21-22, 31

    phone companies, 22–24
    pure VoIP providers, 18–21
    service plans of, 33–34
    softphone providers, 27–29
VoIP services
    additional lines, 93
    blended services, 94
    calling features, 88–93
    fax services, 93
    local number portability, 86–87
    911 activation, 83–86
    service outages, 123
    softphone options, 94–100
    testing process, 100–102
VoIP Wiki, 16, 123, 135
Vonage IP Forum, 123
VoWi-Fi phones, 171–172
    cell phones and, 173–174
    wireless networks and, 172

W

WAN port, 54
wardriving, 158
Web access monitoring, 132
Wi-Fi Protected Access (WPA), 51
Wi-Fi VoIP phones, 171–172
Wikipedia, 16
wikis, 16
WiMax VoIP phones, 172
Wired Equivalent Privacy (WEP), 51
wireless Ethernet bridges, 157
wireless gateways, 51
wireless Internet, 156–158
wireless networks, 129–130, 133, 161
wireless phones, 10, 158, 171
wireless VoIP, 171–172
WPA2 security, 130
WPA-PSK security, 130

X

X-PRO SoftPhone, 95–96, 160

Be Computer Savvy
On-The-Go!

Wi-Fi hot spots, iChat conferencing, AirPort Extreme wireless networks, digital phones, Bluetooth devices, and more—let Peachpit help you stay connected no matter where you're going. If you plan to take your computer on the road, these great books will show you how to do so quickly, effectively, and with minimum hassle and headaches!

Macs on the Go
John Tollett and
Robin Williams
ISBN 0-321-24748-5
$21.99

Global Mobile: Connecting without walls, wires, or borders
Fred Johnson
ISBN 0-321-27871-2
$15.99

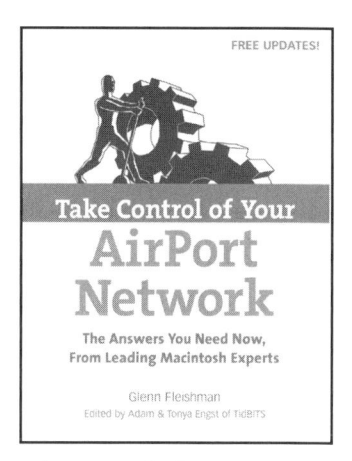

Take Control of Your Airport Network
Glenn Fleishman and
Adam Engst
ISBN 0-321-32116-2
$16.99

Peachpit

www.peachpit.com

Buy 24.99 Slight water damage noted 9/10

621.38212 FIELD
Field, David, 1944 May 25-
Fire the phone company : a
handy guide to voice over
IP

DATE DUE		
SEP 1 3 2006		
DEC 2 9 2007		